# Facilitating in the Classroom

## Practical Tools to Empower Learning

**Ingrid Bens, M.Ed. CPF.**
**Certified Professional Facilitator**

FACILITATING IN THE CLASSROOM

INGRID BENS, M.Ed., CPF.
Published by FACILITATION TUTOR LLC

Editor: Mia Ruggiero
Book Designer: Cindy Readnower
Artwork: Carol Tornatore

Copyright© 2020 by Ingrid Bens
All rights reserved.

No part of this publication may be reproduced, stored in a retrieval system, or transmitted in any from or by any means electronic, mechanical, photocopying, recording, scanning, or otherwise, except as permitted under the United States Copyright Act, without the prior written consent of the author.

Limit of Liability/Disclaimer of Warranty: While the publisher and the author have used their best efforts in preparing this book, they make no representations or warranties with respect to the accuracy or completeness of the contents of this book and specifically disclaim any implied warranties of merchantability or fitness for a particular purpose. No warranty may be created or extended by sales representatives or written sales materials. The advice and strategies contained herein may not be suitable for your situation. You should consult with a professional where appropriate. Neither the publisher nor author shall be liable for any loss of profit or any other commercial damages, including but not limited to special, incidental, consequential, or other damages. Readers should be aware that Internet websites offered as citations and/or sources for further information may have changed or disappeared between the time this was written and when it is read.

Excerpts from this book may be reproduced with permission of the author. Inclusion of significant segments of this book in training manuals can be arranged by contacting the author directly at Ingrid@facilitationtutor.com.

ISBN: 978-0-9970970-2-3
LCCN: 2019920410

Also by Ingrid Bens

**Books**

Facilitating with Ease! 4th ed.
Facilitating IEP Meetings
Advanced Facilitation Skills
Facilitating to Lead
Facilitation Techniques for Consultants
Facilitation at a Glance!
Conflict at a Glance
Team Launch
Advanced Team Facilitation

**Instruments**

The Facilitation Skills Inventory

**Online Courses**

Facilitation Core Skills

**www.facilitationtutor.com**

*Education is not the learning of facts,
but the training of the mind to think.*

Albert Einstein


*The illiterate of the 21$^{st}$ century will be those
who cannot learn, unlearn and relearn.*

Alvin Toffler
*Future Shock*

# Table of Contents

Introduction ................................................................................................. 7
Definitions ................................................................................................. 13

**Chapter One: Origins and Models** ............................................................ 15
   Classroom Origins ................................................................................. 15
   Role Definition ....................................................................................... 16
   The Adult Education Model .................................................................... 19
   Summary of the Variable Roles of the Teacher ...................................... 20
   Changing Student Roles ........................................................................ 21
   Levels of Engagement ............................................................................ 22
   WIIFM: The Key to Engagement ............................................................. 25

**Chapter Two: Facilitation Core Practices** ................................................. 26
   Defining Facilitation ............................................................................... 26
   Comparing Content and Process ........................................................... 27
   Facilitation Core Practices ..................................................................... 28
   Staying Neutral About the Content ........................................................ 30
   The Parameters of Neutrality ................................................................. 30
   Learn to Say *"Okay"* ............................................................................. 31
   Effective Note Taking ............................................................................. 32
   The Rules of Wording ............................................................................ 32
   Final Recording Tip ................................................................................ 33
   Recording Do's and Don'ts .................................................................... 33
   Starting a Facilitation ............................................................................. 34
   During a Facilitation .............................................................................. 35
   What is a Process Check? .................................................................... 35
   Staying on Track ................................................................................... 36
   Ending a Facilitation ............................................................................. 37
   Facilitating Online Learning .................................................................. 38
   The Best and Worst Practices of Facilitators ........................................ 40
   Facilitation at a Glance Cue Card ......................................................... 41

**Chapter Three: Effective Questioning** ..................................................... 42
   The Principles of Effective Questioning ................................................ 42
   Question Types ..................................................................................... 43
   Question Formats ................................................................................. 44
   The Importance of Follow-on Questions .............................................. 45
   Responding to Questions ..................................................................... 45
   Question Cascades .............................................................................. 46
   The 5 Whys .......................................................................................... 47
   Structured Observation Sheets ............................................................ 48
   Sequential Questioning ........................................................................ 48
   The Question Bank .............................................................................. 49
   Questioning Do's and Don'ts ................................................................ 52

**Chapter Four: Decision-Making in the Classroom** .................................. 53
   The Need to Make Group Decisions ................................................... 53
   Non-Decision-Making Conversations .................................................. 53
   Decision-Making Conversations .......................................................... 54
   Decision-Making Options ..................................................................... 55

 *Multi-voting* Variations ............................................................................... 59

## Chapter Five: Facilitating Through Conflict ........................................................ 68
 How Facilitators Manage Conflict ........................................................................ 68
 An Important Tip: Never, Ever Utter the Word Conflict! ..................................... 69
 Group *Norms* ........................................................................................................ 69
 Classroom *Norms* ................................................................................................ 70
 Project Team *Norms* ............................................................................................ 71
 Safety *Norms* ....................................................................................................... 73
 Behavioral Intervention ......................................................................................... 75
 *Norm*-based Interventions ..................................................................................... 77
 Body Language Interventions ............................................................................... 78
 Giving and Receiving Feedback ........................................................................... 80
 Feedback Guidelines ............................................................................................. 81
 Receiving Feedback with Grace ........................................................................... 82

## Chapter Six: Building Strong Teams ................................................................... 84
 Teams Need Structure .......................................................................................... 84
 Team *Storming* ..................................................................................................... 88
 The Team Intervention Model ............................................................................... 88
 The *Performing* Stage .......................................................................................... 91
 *Adjourning* the Team ............................................................................................ 91

## Chapter Seven: Learning Design ......................................................................... 93
 Essential Supplies ................................................................................................ 93
 Physical Layout .................................................................................................... 95
 Ways to Organize Learners ................................................................................. 97
 Engaging Lectures ............................................................................................. 102
 Managing Time ................................................................................................... 109
 Sharing Group Learning .................................................................................... 109

## Chapter Eight: Structured Conversations ........................................................ 112
 Structured Conversation # 1: Sequential Questioning ...................................... 112
 Sequential Questioning Example ...................................................................... 113
 Structured Conversation #2: Constructive Controversy ................................... 114
 Constructive Controversy Topics ...................................................................... 115
 Structured Conversation #3: *SWOT Analysis* .................................................. 116
 Sample *SWOT* Questions .................................................................................. 117
 Structured Conversation #4: *Brainstorming* ..................................................... 119
 Structured Conversation #5: Affinity Diagrams ................................................ 120
 Structured Conversation #6: *Forcefield* Analysis ............................................ 121
 Variations of *Forcefield* Analysis ...................................................................... 122
 Structured Conversation #7: Decision Grids .................................................... 123
 Structured Conversation #8: Surveys ............................................................... 125
 Structured Conversation #9: Systematic Problem Solving .............................. 126
 Sample Problem Solving Topics ....................................................................... 127

## Enhance Your Facilitation Skills ........................................................................ 128

## Annotated Bibliography ...................................................................................... 133

## About the Author/Contributors .......................................................................... 134

## Chapter References ............................................................................................ 135

# Introduction

**Education is in the Midst of an Epic Transformation.**

This transformation has been going on for decades. If you walk into a grade five classroom today, you won't see the straight rows of desks that were the hallmark of learning back in the fifties and sixties. Instead, you'll find desks arranged in clusters. That's because children, in even the earliest grades, have been working in teams and collaborating on projects for decades.

In the classroom of the past, the teacher spoke while students listened. Young people were seen as empty vessels whose heads needed to be filled. Students were discouraged from talking to each other. It was the voice of the teacher that dominated. Students were expected to memorize what was taught, then they were tested. It was a world of rote memorization and regurgitation, a world that is rapidly disappearing.

Recently, technology has unleashed a tsunami of change. Classrooms everywhere are connecting to the internet and students walk around with a computer in their pocket. These computers give them instant access to any topic they care to investigate. Today, even the youngest child can search for information in a vast ocean of data.

And the use of technology is still in its infancy. Most teachers still use class time to lecture, but that could change tomorrow. Many schools already have their own *Learning Management System* or *LMS,* where teachers can post their lectures. When this becomes commonplace, precious classroom time will be freed up for interaction and skill building.

In the meantime, the omnipresence of technology is changing students' perceptions and is even altering their brains. Everything they look at is moving fast. Instead of reading pages of text, they prefer to look at videos. Instead of being passive consumers of entertainment, they engage with the games they play. Interacting with technology has created expectations in them for speed and constant stimulation.

Past generations of learners were conditioned from childhood to sit passively and read: to listen to lectures and take notes. Today's digital generation isn't programmed that way. Without stimulation they disengage.

So, exactly what do today's students need in order to stay tuned in? Activities that move fast, that use technology, that get them interacting.

To create that kind of dynamic learning environment, teachers need to become experts at designing participative classroom activities. These are activities that ensure that students are active partners in learning. Teachers also need to become skilled in the art of facilitation.

## Why Facilitation?

Because facilitating is the opposite of lecturing. Instead of transferring information to learners, facilitative teachers pull insights from them. Instead of focusing on the presentation of facts, facilitative teachers design activities that enable students to discover facts for themselves. On its simplest level, the shift from lecturing to facilitating boils down to the difference between two verbs: telling and asking.

| The Telling Mode (Instructing) | The Asking Mode (Facilitating) |
|---|---|
| - the curriculum is fixed | - the curriculum is dynamic |
| - the teacher knows all | - the teacher knows a lot |
| - learners know very little | - learners know a lot too |
| - the teacher does all the talking | - learners explore, then interpret their findings |
| - learners need to listen, take notes and memorize | - learners engage in discussions |
| - the teacher tests retention and comprehension | - the teacher helps learners integrate their new knowledge |

In the facilitative classroom, the teacher creates structured experiences. The students join groups to conduct research, take part in role-plays, have discussions or conduct experiments. The teacher then helps them interpret their findings, corrects their mistakes and fills information gaps.

## What is Facilitation?

Facilitation is a specific set of techniques for managing both dialogue and group dynamics. Facilitating in the classroom requires competency in two distinct areas:

1. **Core facilitation skills:** This is a defined set of facilitation techniques that are used to manage group discussions. It includes techniques to solicit ideas, create participation, make notes and manage group dynamics.

2. **Experiential learning design:** This is the design of complex, interactive learning activities in step-by-step detail, which includes how students should be divided, which activities will be used and how findings will be debriefed.

**Note:** In this book a number of terms are used Interchangeably. These include: adult education, *Andragogy*, experiential learning, facilitated learning, participative learning, engaged learning, empowered learning, action learning and student-led learning.

## The Benefits of Experiential Learning

Participative activities generate a number of benefits. These vary by group, of course, since learners always bring their unique perspectives. A few of the most notable benefits are:

- it's active: learners are up and doing
- engaged students are more energetic and interested
- it utilizes all four learning styles since all of the senses are involved
- participation and engagement encourage buy-in
- it builds research, analysis and discussion skills
- learners who work together build social skills
- it brings many perspectives into the discussion
- it brings real-world relevance into the classroom
- it encourages personal growth and development.

The result of properly designed experiential learning is that participants become more capable of critical thought and independent action. This helps them to become life-long learners.

## The Downside of Experiential Learning

It would be wrong to tout the benefits of participative learning without pointing out that there are a number of drawbacks. These include that:

- exploration and reflection take longer than giving a lecture
- some learners may not be capable of learning independently
- groups work at different speeds so it's a challenge to manage class time
- teachers give up a measure of control when they empower students to find their own information and draw their own conclusions
- the quality of the learning experience will vary between groups, resulting in differences in both the content learned and the skills acquired
- learners may generate flawed or incomplete information
- active learning isn't effective if the learning activity is poorly designed
- teachers who are new to facilitation will need to master a new set of skills.

Teachers who use participative approaches know only too well that learners can sometimes head in an unexpected direction. These side-trips can lead to powerful insights or they may lead to dead ends. Given the potential for students to veer off the designated path, participative learning only works for teachers who are willing to accept a degree of uncertainty in order to achieve increased engagement.

## Lectures Are Still Important

It would be easy to conclude from all this, that lectures are frowned upon in the participative classroom. This is far from the truth. Providing instruction and conducting demonstrations will always be an essential part of the teaching process. This is especially true when the material is complex, or when learners need a detailed explanation of a new concept. Lectures can, however, be made less static and more engaging by applying the facilitation techniques described throughout this book.

In many cases, lectures simply need to be repositioned within the learning model. In the conventional approach to teaching, learning begins with the presentation of content. In the experiential learning model, lectures take place after students have first explored a topic for themselves. By then, the learners feel that they're already somewhat familiar with the subject, which deepens their interest. Becoming a facilitative teacher does not mean giving up lecturing. It simply means relocating lectures and using them in a new way.

The bottom line is that instructing and facilitating aren't competing approaches. There will always be times when it's best to simply present information and other times when it's more effective to engage students in the discovery process.

> Think of instructing and facilitating as two gears in the same gearbox. Both are important and each has its place.
>
> | Lecture in order to… | Facilitate in order to… |
> |---|---|
> | - explain a new concept | - enable personal goal setting |
> | - describe a complex theory | - encourage exploration |
> | - provide an example | - spark thoughtful reflection |
> | - demonstrate a correct practice | - stimulate critical thinking |
> | - correct learner mistakes | - manage group discussions |
> | - fill in learning gaps | - connect ideas |

When teachers develop their facilitation skills, they gain the capacity to create an effective blend of expert instruction and learner-centered exploration.

*Introduction*

## What's in This Book?

Although the practice of facilitation was created within the field of Adult Education, it quickly migrated into corporations, government agencies and the social sector. There, the practice matured and evolved. This book aims to bring what's been learned in those settings back to the classroom.

**Chapter One** provides context for experiential learning by sharing key models and definitions. It describes the steps in the experiential learning model and outlines how teacher roles shift in and out of facilitation at various stages in the experiential learning model. It also provides clarity about the difference between classroom facilitation and group facilitation. Since experiential learning can be implemented at varying levels of empowerment, these too are described in this chapter. Also included is an overview of the impact of experiential learning on students.

**Chapter Two** describes the main tools and techniques that are needed to facilitate group discussions. It offers an overview of the core competencies and gives examples of how specific facilitation techniques can be applied in the classroom. It details how to facilitate the beginning, middle, and end of group discussions. Also provided are strategies for staying neutral and recording group ideas. This chapter ends with a brief discussion about how to adapt facilitation for online learning.

**Chapter Three** explores how teachers can use questioning to stimulate thought. It provides general guidance on various question types and formats. There is also a brief exploration of the facilitative teacher's use of questioning which differs from how questions are traditionally handled in the classroom. A collection of sample questions is included at the end of this chapter.

**Chapter Four** provides tools that enable group decision making. These methods engage students in such activities as priority setting, ranking and evaluating. The techniques discussed include consensus building, compromise, one-person decisions, *Majority Voting,* and *Multi-voting.* Since *Multi-voting* is so useful in groups, this chapter features over ten ways to structure a group decision process.

**Chapter Five** illustrates the techniques facilitators use to prevent and manage conflict. It includes sections on how to utilize *Norming* to create a harmonious climate, how to intervene when behaviors become ineffective, and the optimal way to give and receive feedback. These techniques are positioned within the core approach that facilitators use when individual or group conflict crops up.

**Chapter Six** provides strategies for building and maintaining effective teams. It describes the stages of team development: *Forming, Storming, Norming* and *Performing.* It outlines the key conversations that need to be facilitated in order to launch a new team. Detailed intervention strategies for rescuing teams that encounter turbulence are also offered.

*Facilitating in the Classroom*

**Chapter Seven** delves into how facilitative teachers design and then manage classroom activities. It provides multiple examples of how participative activities can be used to turn lectures into active learning. This chapter also describes numerous ways of organizing students into learning teams.

**Chapter Eight** describes some of the most useful structured conversations for classroom use. Step-by-step instructions are provided for tools like *Sequential Questioning, Constructive Controversy, SWOT Analysis, Brainstorming, Forcefield Analysis,* and *Systematic Problem Solving.* These processes can form the foundation for entire classes or be used online to encourage group collaboration.

Since no single volume can do everything, this book does not attempt to lay out every possible group activity, from warm-up games, to role-plays, to case studies and simulations. Fortunately, there are many great books out there that describe these important elements. Refer to the annotated bibliography on page 133 for the names of a few recommended titles.

Whether you're already an experienced classroom facilitator or are relatively new to the practice, I'm confident that this book will help you to further elevate your practice.

*Ingrid Bens, M.Ed.*
*Certified Professional Facilitator*

# Definitions

**Facilitation:** An approach to group management that's based on asking instead of telling. Facilitators provide structure and then keep discussions focused to ensure a high-quality outcome.

**Facilitator:** A neutral helper and enabler whose goal is to support others as they pursue their objectives. Facilitators deliberately stay out of the conversation to ensure that group members are taking the lead.

**Facilitative Teacher:** Someone who applies the technique of facilitation to learning design and classroom management in order to create an engaged learning environment.

**Structured Experiences:** Learning activities that are designed in step-by-step detail.

**The Socratic Method:** An early approach to facilitative teaching attributed to the Greek philosopher Socrates, famous for asking challenging questions to spark debate and encourage inquiry.

**Pedagogy:** While this term is commonly used to describe the discipline that deals with the theory and practice of teaching, the origin of the term actually derives from the ancient Greek word *"peda"* which means child and *"agogos"* meaning leader. Taken together pedagogy translates as "to lead a child". In this book the term *pedagogy* is used in this original context to refer to the methods used to teach children.

**Andragogy:** This term refers to methods and principles used in adult education. The concept was first articulated in the 1800's and later made popular in the United States by educator Malcolm Knowles. The term is a combination of the ancient Greek words *"andr"* meaning *"man"* and *"agogos"* meaning *"leader of"*. Andragogy literally means "*to lead a man.*"

**Plenary:** A large group session held to share the ideas previously developed in sub-groups.

***Norms*:** A set of rules or guidelines created by group members that everyone in the group agrees to follow. Often referred to as rules of conduct.

## Questions Answered in This Book

How is education changing?

How are today's learners different?

Why is facilitation important?

What is facilitation?

Why should teachers use facilitation?

What are the benefits of facilitating in the classroom?

What are the drawbacks of facilitating in the classroom?

How is experiential learning different?

Do teachers really need to be neutral?

What are the core tools and techniques of facilitation?

Why is questioning so important?

How do facilitative teachers handle questions?

How can facilitative teachers create participation?

How do facilitators manage conflict?

How do you build and maintain healthy project teams?

How can learners take part in decision making?

How can lectures be more interactive?

What are some different ways of debriefing a learning activity?

What are some ways to structure group discussions?

# Chapter One: Origins and Models

Before we dive into when and how to use facilitation in the classroom, it's important to explore core concepts and tools. To accomplish this, chapter one will:

- describe the origins of the practice of facilitation
- explain that adult education methods are not just for adults
- examine differences between group facilitators and facilitative teachers
- explain the steps in the Adult Education Model
- describe the different roles of the teacher in experiential learning
- explain how experiential learning changes student roles
- define the various levels of engagement in the classroom
- explain why learner buy-in is critically important

## Classroom Origins

Facilitation originated inside the field of adult education as the teaching method best suited to support adults in their learning journey. The model used in experiential learning design was made popular by American educator Malcolm Knowles who postulated that:

- **Adults learn only what they feel they need to learn** – Adults want to know how a topic relates to them and their goals.
- **Adults learn by doing** - Adults prefer to learn through practice and participation, so that they can develop new skills.
- **Adults learn best in an informal setting** - Adults learn best in an inviting and collaborative environment.
- **Adults want to be equal partners in the process** - Adults want to choose options based on their needs and the impact a topic could provide.
- **Adults want to engage with each other** - Socialization is important to adults who want to make and strengthen connections.
- **Adults want to feel valued** - Adults learn best in an environment that emphasizes self-worth and dignity.
- **Adults want trust** – Adults learn best when they're in an atmosphere that encourages them to make mistakes and try again.
- **Adult learning focuses on problem solving** - Adults prefer posing and answering realistic questions to gain more understanding.
- **Adults want relevance** - The adult's orientation to learning is chiefly related to application.

## Not Just for Adults

Although *Andragogy* was created to meet the needs of mature students, it has been shown to work with younger age groups as long as they are:

- open and curious
- internally motivated to learn
- able to collaborate with others on assignments
- capable of searching for information, assessing data, and reflecting on what they've discovered
- sufficiently disciplined to work independently

When these traits are present in youngsters, *Adult Education* methods are not only effective, but are often the only way to get students to really engage.

# Role Definition

Shortly after it was created inside the field of adult education, facilitation migrated into the workplace. There it evolved into an important set of tools for managing meetings, leading teams, mediating conflict and structuring complex conversations. Here's a brief look at the differences between the roles of group facilitator and facilitative teacher.

## The Group Facilitator

A group facilitator is someone who designs and then manages structured conversations with the aim of enabling groups to make high quality decisions.

<u>The goal of group facilitators is to help group members access their inner resources in order to make collaborative decisions and identify next steps.</u>

Group facilitators are typically outsiders. Groups will hire an external facilitator when they need the help of a neutral party to help them sort out a complex issue. During a facilitation event, decision-making power resides with group members. Group facilitators never impose their ideas on their clients.

Since group facilitators have no authority over their clients, it's easy for them to stay neutral about whatever the group decides. This neutrality frees them to focus on providing the structure needed to ensure a thorough and comprehensive thought process.

Rather than being a player, group facilitators act more like referees: watching the action more than participating in it. They help members define their goals, they ensure that group members have effective rules to guide interactions, they provide an orderly sequence of activities, they keep their finger on the pulse, and know when to move on or wrap things up, they keep discussions focused, resolve conflicts and help members achieve closure.

*Chapter One: Origins and Models*

Here is a list of typical group facilitator activities:

- conducting background research to understand the needs of the client, and what they hope to achieve
- creating a detailed meeting design to guide discussions
- helping the group clarify its overall goal, as well as its specific objectives
- preparing a detailed agenda that includes process notes that describe how the discussion will unfold
- helping the group create rules of conduct that encourage effective behaviors
- ensuring that assumptions are surfaced and tested
- questioning and probing to stimulate deeper exploration
- offering the right tools and techniques when they're needed
- encouraging equal participation by all
- keeping group discussion on track
- making notes that accurately reflect the ideas of group members
- helping members constructively manage differences of opinion
- redirecting ineffective behaviors
- offering ways to move past roadblocks
- providing feedback to the group, so that they can assess their progress and make adjustments
- helping the group make decisions, achieve closure, and identify next steps
- helping members access resources both from inside and outside the group

Group facilitators work with all group sizes, from the five members of an executive committee, to the ten members of a project team, to fifty citizens taking part in a planning forum. Some examples of the types of discussions group facilitators are asked to lead include team building, strategic planning, project launch, risk assessment, priority-setting, project update, problem solving, process improvement, project debrief, conflict mediation, focus group discussion and community planning.

**The Facilitative Teacher**

When teachers facilitate, they adhere to the same beliefs and use the same core tools used by group facilitators. They also model the same behaviors and use the same language.

Despite these similarities, classroom facilitation has a very different goal. Instead of being aimed at enabling decision making and action planning, the purpose of classroom facilitation is to support learners in pursuing knowledge and acquiring skills.

Another difference is that the facilitative teacher is almost always a permanent member of the group. They also have point of view and subject matter expertise. Even more

*Facilitating in the Classroom*

significant is the fact that teachers have direct authority over the people they're facilitating. Despite these differences, facilitative teachers also use neutrality, although they use it to encourage students to reach their own conclusions.

Facilitative teachers design learning activities, organize sub-groups and monitor activities. At the end of exploration activities, they facilitate discussions so that learners can reflect on what they've discovered. They remain neutral during this phase so as not to interfere with the learners' thought processes.

Once learners have fully mined their experience, the facilitative teacher steps out of the neutral role to add theory, offer expertise, fill in gaps, and correct mistaken conclusions. This is when they lecture and answer direct questions. After lecturing, the teacher once again plays the facilitator role to help learners figure out how they can use their newfound knowledge. This closure is essential. For more about these shifts in and out of the facilitator role see pages 19 and 20.

**Comparing Group Facilitators and Facilitative Teachers:**

| The Group Facilitator | The Facilitative Teacher |
|---|---|
| -Is an outsider | - Is an insider |
| -Has no authority over group members | - Has authority over learners |
| -Is there temporarily | - Stays with the learners |
| -Designs structured conversations | - Structures learning activities |
| -Manages discussions | - Manages discussions |
| -Offers decision-making tools | - Offers decision-making tools |
| -Manages group dynamics | - Manages group dynamics |
| -Never offers opinions | - Adds theory and fills in gaps |
| -Helps groups plan next steps | - Helps learners connect ideas |

*Adapted from the Monograph entitled "Facilitative Leadership" prepared for the *National Institute for School Leadership (NISL)* by Ingrid Bens, M.Ed. 2015.

*Chapter One: Origins and Models*

# The Adult Education Model

Experiential learning *or Andragogy* is managed differently from traditional learning. Instead of starting by sharing information, the Adult Education Model begins with either research, a role-play, an experiment, or structured observation that provides a hands-on experience with the subject. After the experience is complete, the teacher facilitates a group discussion to help learners reflect on what their experience has taught them.

After the learners' insights have been fully exploited, the teacher slips into instructor mode to add content. Having heard what the learners discovered, the teacher can build on those insights, fill in gaps, and correct mistaken conclusions. The teacher can do this by giving a lecture or demonstrating a skill.

To complete the learning cycle, the teacher facilitates a conversation to help learners connect what they learned to other topics or situations. The teacher remains neutral during the application discussions.

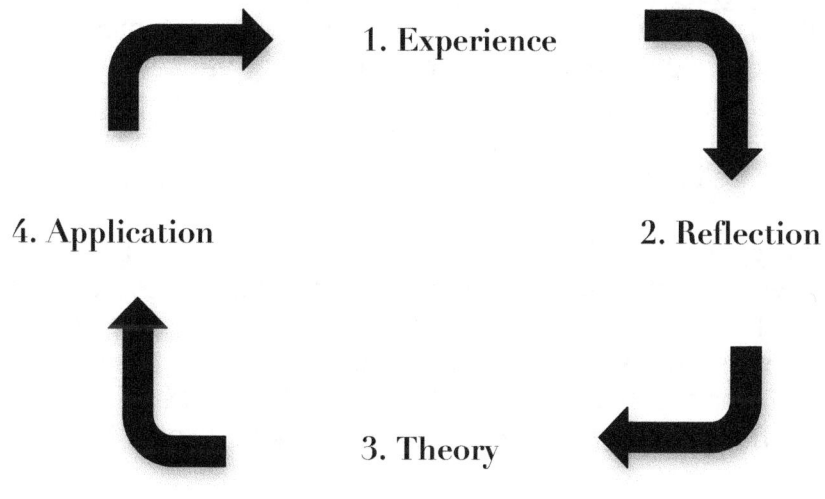

Malcolm Knowles, 1975

It is important to note that these components don't always unfold exactly in the order shown in the model. Sometimes a facilitative teacher will give a brief lecture to set the context for the experience phase. If students are working remotely, they may view an online lecture before taking part in an activity. The important point to remember is that the experience and reflection elements are key to the participative approach to learning, regardless of when they take place.

*Facilitating in the Classroom*

## Summary of the Variable Roles of the Teacher

During participative learning, teachers switch in and out of the following roles.

**Pre-class Activity Designer:** In advance of a participative class, the teacher sets the learning objectives, assesses the content to be taught, then designs activities such as role plays, simulations, small group discussions and research assignments. The teacher assembles the supplies and props needed to conduct the activity and creates clear step-by-step instructions.

**Experience Phase Activity Coordinator:** At the start of the experience phase, the teacher explains the process, divides the students into groups, and distributes the materials needed for the experience. While students are busy with the activity, the teacher monitors progress and manages time. At this point, the teacher focuses on managing the process and does not offer content.

**Reflection Phase Facilitator:** When the experience is over, the teacher steps into the role of neutral facilitator, leading discussions, managing participation, and posing questions that encourage deeper exploration. The facilitative teacher asks questions to challenge learner conclusions and to stimulate debate. By staying neutral, they encourage learners to be analytical and self-reliant. If the teacher does interject bits of information at this stage, it's only done to stimulate further student thought.

**Theory Phase Instructor:** Once learners have fully exploited their insights, the teacher stops facilitating and switches into lecture mode in order to share key concepts. At this point, the teacher is no longer neutral, since the theory being shared is likely the result of considerable research and therefore, not open to debate. During this phase, students are able to augment or correct their own conclusions. If the students' work has been thorough, they will feel that they already understand the salient points of the lesson.

**Application Phase Facilitator:** When the lecture is over, the teacher switches back to neutral facilitator mode to lead discussions, during which students discuss how the relevance of that they learned to other topics or to their lives. Neutrality is appropriate here since the application of knowledge tends to be personal.

These role shifts highlight the fact that teachers who use facilitation in the classroom don't use it all the time. They switch in and out of the role, depending on which segment of the learning cycle is taking place.

### Variable Teacher Roles

```
Pre-class – Preparation........Activity designer
Phase 1   – Experience........Activity coordinator
Phase 2   – Reflection..........Neutral facilitator
Phase 3   – Theory..............Lecturer
Phase 4   – Application........Neutral facilitator
```

## Changing Student Roles

The shift to experiential learning changes student roles as well. Instead of being mostly consumers of learning, they become active generators of knowledge. Instead of only being taught, they also teach others.

After some exposure to being facilitated, students will inevitably learn how to facilitate themselves. Learning to facilitate can take time. Once mastered, however, this new skill helps students run small group discussions and project meetings more effectively.

Since so much experiential learning takes place in project teams, students have the opportunity to develop project management skills. They learn to keep activities on schedule and on track. Furthermore, for project teams to work harmoniously, students need to be able to both give and receive specific feedback. Below is a brief summary of a few of the roles that students play in a participative classroom.

**Classroom managers:** Since a classroom might be rearranged several times a day, it's necessary that students play a major role in setting up and taking down various classroom configurations. This includes moving furniture, posting newsprint, organizing supplies and recording notes.

**Researchers:** Students play a major role in conducting research and compiling information. They do this both independently and as members of learning teams.

**Experts:** Students who develop real depth about specific topics can be tapped to make presentations, create displays or broadcast on the school website.

**Teachers:** Having developed expertise on a topic, students don't just make presentations. They also do peer coaching and tutoring. This deepens learning since nothing helps you learn about a topic like teaching it to someone else.

**Facilitators:** In order to have effective small group discussions, students need to learn to acquire facilitation skills. This is easy once they've seen their teachers in action.

**Team Player:** Students in the experiential classroom play an active role in setting both classroom and project team *Norms*. When their teams veer off track they know how to give and receive feedback, so that issues can be addressed.

## Levels of Engagement

It is very important to note that experiential learning can be implemented to different degrees.

As you read the following examples, notice that each approach engages learners differently. Some of the variables to consider when deciding which level is appropriate include the age of the learners, their ability to work independently, their capacity to analyze and assess data, the time available, and the size of the group.

**Example:** Teaching students about the four stages of team development: *Forming, Storming, Norming* and *Performing.*

### Level 1 – The Participative Lecture Approach

- The teacher gives a brief overview of the subject. Only enough information is provided about the four stages of team development to give a clear context for the remainder of the lecture.
- Learners are formed into dyads or triads to identify the questions they're seeking answers to, from the lecture. They write their questions down, but don't share them with the whole class.
- The teacher gives the lecture about the four stages of team development.
- The teacher opens the floor for students to read their questions, and to share any answers that they've already gleaned from the lecture.
- The teacher facilitates that discussion by asking if anyone else had that same question and inviting them to join the conversation.
- The teacher invites learners to answer any of their classmates' unanswered questions. If no answers are forthcoming from the students, the teacher provides answers.

### Level 2 – The Group Discussion Approach

- Learners are given pre-reading about the four-team development stages.
- At the start of the workshop, learners read a case study about a project team preparing an entry for a regional science fair. The team in the case study experiences major conflict just a few weeks after forming. The project they're running spins out of control.
- Learners are divided into sub-groups to discuss a set of questions about team development that have been prepared by the teacher. These include: *"What was it like during the first few weeks in the life of the team? Why did people get along? What happened to create conflict? How did members react? How did the leader react? What mistakes were made? What could the team leader have done to resolve conflicts and get the team back on track?"*
- The workshop leader invites the sub-groups to share their insights with the whole class. During this discussion, the teacher neutrally asks questions, makes

*Chapter One: Origins and Models*

suggestions for the learners to consider. They then help the groups to formulate an overall intervention strategy.
- The leader then gives a lecture about a variety of intervention approaches useful to resolve team storming.
- Students compare the ideas presented in the lecture with the intervention strategies that they developed earlier. Learners are given an opportunity to adjust and improve their original strategies.
- Learners are invited to reflect on when and how they can apply what they've learned should they encounter conflict in a project or sports team.

**Level 3 – The Dynamic Experience Approach**

- Learners are invited to share why they feel that teambuilding is relevant to them and their project work. During this session, they're also asked to write down what they most want to learn about how teams work, plus one question that they personally need to have answered about how teams develop and grow.
- Learners are formed into teams of six to ten people. They're given an outline of the steps needed to effectively launch a new team. They are also given a set of specific questions that they must answer together. An example of these questions is provided on page 85. Team members take part in a discussion to identify a team goal and objectives, a set of team rules, and criteria for selecting a team leader. They then use their criteria to pick a leader for the upcoming activity.
- The team formation activity is debriefed in order to get member insights about their experience with team start up. They're also asked to identify what each dialogue achieved. The newly formed teams are then given a deliberately difficult decision-making challenge that generates a bit of conflict. This mild friction gives the students a taste of some of the dilemmas that are part of what's known as *The Storming Phase* of team growth. They might argue, divide into cliques, and fail to achieve the task. In *Storming*, it's common for people to challenge the leader and for people to ignore the team rules.
- At the end of that tempestuous experience, the workshop leader provides a process tool known as *Forcefield Analysis*, which you can find on page 121. This tool consists of a chart with columns for three questions:

    1. "What did we do well during the challenge"? (Show as chart)
    2. "What didn't we do so well during the challenge?"
    3. "What do we need to do to about what we didn't do so well?"

- Each team appoints a neutral facilitator to help group members answer the three questions. When they're done, the group uses *Multi-voting* (page 59) to identify the strategies that have the most potential to resolve *Storming*.
- To complete the intervention, each person privately writes out what they will personally do differently to ensure team success.
- Team members are then invited to read out their personal change commitment.

*Facilitating in the Classroom*

- The teacher then presents a brief lecture on the theory of team development stages. This is a participative lecture, during which the instructor periodically asks questions to draw out learner insights.
- The teacher facilitates a further discussion in which team members talk about how they can use what they learned in sports and project teams.
- To end the session, learners privately assess the extent to which the class met their personal learning goal, and whether or not their most important questions have been answered. The teachers then facilitates a discussion that lets people share what they learned.

**Level 4 – The Total Immersion Approach**

- Students who are working on a project together are facilitated through a team formation activity (page 85). This project could be planning the spring prom, working on the school newsletter, or planning a special event. The nature of the actual activity is immaterial, as long as the team meets on a regular basis, and is going to stay together for at least three months.
- After about six weeks, or if the team starts to show signs of *Storming*, the teacher who is overseeing the project conducts the team improvement exercises described starting on page 88.
- In a few weeks, the teacher checks in with individual team members to determine if the sources of *Storming* have been resolved.
- If the team experiences another *Storming* phase, the teacher repeats the team intervention activities.

## W.I.F.M. - The Key to Engagement

Regardless of which level of engagement is being deployed, facilitative teachers always strive to create learner buy-in. This is achieved by helping students identify what's in it for them. This buy-in can be on the micro-level or on the macro-level. Here's what that means.

**Micro-level Buy-in** - This refers to buy-in about a specific topic. This is easy to do. At the start of an activity, ask students questions like:

1. "What interests you personally about this topic."
2. "How could learning about this topic help you in the future?"

Invite a few students to share their personal buy-in. This will help others who couldn't think of anything to connect with the topic. At the end of a learning activity, invite students to talk about whether or not they got what they were hoping to gain.

**Macro-level Buy-in** – This is buy-in that connects a person to an entire field of study, often referred to as *Visioning*. This technique involves asking a series of structured questions that help individuals set long-term goals related to the subject or field of study.

Below is a sample set of *Visioning* questions:

*"Imagine that it's seven years from now and you've graduated from this program. Everything that you worked for has worked out beautifully. You could not be happier!*

- *"Where are you working? Is it a big office or are you working at home?"*
- *"What's your job? What does your daily schedule look like?"*
- *"What does your workspace look like?"*
- *"What kinds of projects are you working on?"*
- *"How much are you earning?"*
- *"Who are you working with?"*
- *"What do you love most about your job?"*

Notice that this isn't the old: *"Where do you see yourself in five years?"* which asks people to look forward from the present. Visioning is different. It invites people to imagine that they're actually already in the future. It then asks a series of questions that challenge them to picture themselves doing specific activities. This level of detail encourages use of the side of their brain where images are stored. This is where dreams live. *Visioning* encourages people to connect on a deeper and more personal level.

Facilitative teachers always ensure that every student has a personal vision and that they understand how what they're learning connects to their long-term goals.

*Facilitating in the Classroom*

# Chapter Two: Facilitation Core Practices

Effective engaged learning depends on the mastery of core facilitation skills. These skills have been refined over decades of practice. To outline the core practices, chapter two will:

- define the core principles underpinning the practice
- describe the content/process model
- review the ten core practices
- review the parameters of neutrality
- examine the rules of note taking
- describe recording do's and don'ts
- explain what facilitators do at the beginning, middle, and end of a facilitation
- review facilitation best practices

## Defining Facilitation

The term *Facilitation* comes from the word *facile*; which means "*easy to do*". The term facilitator originated within the field of *Adult Education* where it was coined to describe the role teachers play when they make it easy for learners to deepen their knowledge, without telling them what to think.

Facilitation is a helping function based on:

- asking instead of telling
- listening more than speaking
- posing questions instead of making statements
- drawing ideas from others instead of imposing them

Facilitation is a mindset. All facilitators believe that two heads are better than one: that people gain from working in groups because they benefit from the knowledge of others. Facilitators also believe that encouraging people to think for themselves and take responsibility, motivates them to take on a leadership role in their own lives.

In addition, facilitators believe that:

- all voices should be heard
- everyone's ideas can add value
- everybody gains from the sharing of knowledge and resources
- people are more committed to plans that they've helped to create

## Comparing Content and Process

The two words you'll hear often when facilitation is being described are <u>Content</u> and <u>Process.</u>

In the classroom, the content is the subject matter being taught. It's the facts, skills, or abilities that are part of the lesson. The Content is <u>what</u> is taught. In the past teachers focused mainly on preparing content and then lecturing.

In contrast, process refers to <u>how</u> the class is organized and managed. It includes the methods, procedures, format and tools used. The Process also includes the style of the interaction, the group dynamics, and the climate that's established. It's how the content is taught. In the participative classroom, the teacher is focused on the process whenever they're preparing a step-by-step design for the lesson, or acting as the facilitator during discussions.

| The Content | The Process |
|---|---|
| **What** | **How** |
| The central facts | The learning design |
| The core concepts | The tools being used |
| The main theories | The rules set by the group |
| The requisite skills | The group interaction |
| The facts to be tested | The style of the teacher |

During any experiential learning activity, the teacher switches back and forth between acting as an expert (the content role) and acting as a facilitator (the process role). For more about exactly when and how these shifts take place see page 20.

It's important to note that while facilitators are leading discussions, they stay completely neutral about the content, but remain very assertive about the process. How does that look?

> The teacher doesn't interfere with the thought processes of the students, but actively manages the learning activity and group interaction.

It's a mistake to translate being unassertive about the content, to also being loose about the process. Facilitative teachers never hesitate to decide who's in which group, enforce classroom rules, or intervene if an activity isn't working. They know that failing to be assertive about the process invites disorganization and chaos.

## Facilitation Core Practices

Regardless of the topic under discussion, facilitators never stop doing the following ten things:

**1. Stay Neutral on the Content**

The whole purpose of facilitating is to hear from others, so staying out of the conversation is the hallmark of the facilitator role. Instead of trying to influence what learners think, the facilitative teacher stays focused on providing structure and helping group members explore and analyze on their own. When facilitators ask questions, or offer helpful suggestions, they never do this to impose their views or negate student ideas. Since teachers are not traditionally neutral about content, please read the section later in this chapter about when and how to use neutrality.

**2. Listen Actively**

Since facilitating is all about getting others to talk, listening is key. Active listening is listening to understand, rather than judge. It also means using attentive body language and looking participants in the eye while they're speaking. Listening actively while students present ideas sends the message that their insights are valued.

**3. Ask Questions**

Questioning is the most fundamental facilitator tool. Questions are used to clarify ideas, probe for hidden information, challenge assumptions or ratify a consensus. Effective questioning encourages people to look past symptoms to get at root causes. There is much more about when and how to use questioning effectively in the next chapter.

**4. Paraphrase Continuously**

The only real proof that you've actually heard what someone said is to be able to accurately repeat their comments. For this reason, facilitators paraphrase continuously during discussions. Paraphrasing involves accurately repeating what others say. This lets students know that they were heard and acknowledges their input. Paraphrasing also enables others to hear points for a second time.

**5. Summarize Discussions**

Facilitators summarize the ideas shared by group members at the end of every discussion. They do this to ensure that everyone heard all of the ideas that were shared, to check for accuracy, and to bring closure. Facilitators also summarize in the middle of discussions to catch everyone up on the conversation. Summarizing can also be useful to restart a stalled discussion. In these instances, summarizing reminds people of the points already presented, which often sparks new thinking.

*Chapter Two: Facilitation Core Practices*

### 6. Record Ideas
When a discussion is unfolding, facilitators make accurate notes. They do this on flip chart paper, or on a whiteboard, rather than on notepaper. This lets people see that their ideas are being recorded and helps focus the conversation. Read further on in this chapter for specific tips about how to record group thoughts.

### 7. Synthesize Ideas

When one person makes a point, facilitators bounce it around the group to get others into the conversation. Facilitators do this to combine differing perspectives and so that they can create a summary that reflects the thinking of more than just one person.

### 8. Keep Discussions on Track

If discussions veer off track or lose focus, facilitators notice this and point it out. They place a *Parking Lot* sheet on a side wall and offer participants the option of parking extraneous topics for later discussion. There is more about how to keep discussions focused later in this chapter.

### 9. Test Assumptions

At the start of every discussion, facilitators ask probing questions to make sure that everyone understands the ideas being discussed. They also often ask what the speaker means when they make a point to ensure that they've understood correctly. They also invite people to speak up anytime they're confused about a topic.

### 10. Make Periodic Process Checks

Every now and then facilitators stop the action to check on whether the discussion is still effective. They ask if the purpose is still clear to everyone, if the process is understood, if the pace is too fast or too slow, and to find out how people are feeling. The four elements of process checking are described further on.

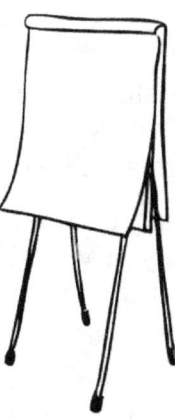

*Facilitating in the Classroom*

## Staying Neutral About the Content

Since neutrality is such a key feature of facilitation, you may be wondering how teachers can possibly stay neutral when they're responsible for delivering content. Here are some points to keep in mind:

1. You're not going to be neutral all the time. You will only refrain from adding content and answering content questions while learners are actively engaged in exploring or thinking things through for themselves.

2. Staying neutral doesn't mean withholding information or failing to correct mistakes. It just means refraining from doing that while students are still actively engaged in a learning activity. At the conclusion of that exploration, teachers can and should provide facts that were missed, as well as correct any mistakes that were made.

3. Always be clear about when you are facilitating. Slipping in and out of the neutral role to chip in ideas can make your efforts at facilitation look manipulative: on the one hand you say you want to hear from them, but then you constantly interject ideas that preempt students from forming their own conclusions.

## The Parameters of Neutrality

One of the most pervasive misconceptions about staying neutral is that you aren't allowed to offer any opinions or give direction. Staying neutral is actually more about not overruling or preempting the thinking of others.

That leaves you a lot of room to use your expertise. For example, you can ask probing questions and even offer helpful ideas for learners to consider. The bottom line is that you can add your ideas while facilitating, as long as you do it in such a way that students feel you're helping them think more deeply. Here are some strategies you can use to offer your expertise without losing your neutrality.

## 1st Strategy—Ask Questions

If you have an idea that can help the students with their research or analysis, or if you sense that the group is overlooking an important idea, you don't have to hold back. Instead, introduce your idea in the form a question that sparks deeper thought.

> **Example:** If learners are missing the idea that weather can play a major role in the outcome of a war, you will still be neutral if you ask: *"What effect did the weather have on the outcome of the war? Was one side better prepared to handle bad weather?"*

Neutrality is preserved because you didn't offer your opinion that weather was a factor, you simply asked questions that encourage a new line of inquiry.

## 2nd Strategy—Offer Suggestions

Another way to share an idea while remaining neutral is to offer a suggestion for consideration. The key is to ensure that the tone of voice being used makes it sound like you're simply putting something on the table for them to think about and not like you're telling them what to think.

> **Example:** *"Take a few minutes to discuss how the time of year selected for the launch of the invasion ended up being a factor."*

As with questioning, neutrality is preserved when making a suggestion, because you aren't dictating learner conclusions.

## 3rd Strategy—Take Off the Facilitator's Hat

If students are presenting mistaken information, you can make an immediate correction. Facilitators try to avoid this type of interjection, but they will do it to save a group from going down the wrong track. When you do this, announce that you're stepping out of the facilitator role:

> **Example:** *"I need to put on my expert hat for a minute to point out that the invasion was not launched in the summer, but in late fall."*

Take off the facilitator hat only when the group is making a mistake that needs to be corrected immediately. If you do it too much, however, you will be sending the message that you lack confidence in the learners' ability to think independently.

## Learn to Say *"Okay"*

Teachers are programmed to be supportive. As soon as they hear a good idea they want to offer congratulations. This is fine in instructor mode, but will not work when facilitating. That's because congratulating implies judging and is therefore, not neutral.

This seems like a picky point, but it's very important. If you tell someone that their idea is a good one, you might be stopping someone else from offering a counter point. Congratulating also makes you sound like you're judging, when you ought to be encouraging students to judge for themselves. Remember that your position power will turn any assessments that you make into facts.

- When students bring up what seems like an excellent point, instead of saying things like, *"Good point,"* or *"Great idea."* Train yourself to say, *"Okay."*
- Saying, *"Okay,"* let's you acknowledge that you've heard an idea, but doesn't indicate your approval or judgment.
- In that same vein, whenever you're tempted to say, *"I like that idea,"* substitute, *"Do the rest of you like that idea?"* After all, facilitators don't judge ideas as much as they help people make those assessments for themselves.

*Facilitating in the Classroom*

## Effective Note Taking

Facilitation is closely identified with those awkward three-legged easels that are the trademark of the profession. Flip charts were invented by the first facilitators who were looking for a way to help group members keep track of discussions.

When you record what's said, learners see immediate proof that their input has been heard and captured. On top of that, writing on a flip chart or whiteboard lets you use pictures, charts, and graphs.

Recording in front of the group requires slightly larger handwriting, so that the words can be seen from the back of the classroom. Many people try to get out of acting as the recorder by claiming that their handwriting is messy. Since very few people have perfect handwriting, you'll need to encourage everybody to relax about it.

You may also be wondering if it's really necessary to write on a flip chart or whiteboard while you're facilitating. The simple answer is yes. It really is important to record ideas, especially if the notes are needed for further action.

## The Rules of Wording

Whenever you're recording student ideas, it's important to write down what they say without editing too much. If you change too many words, or add words that you personally prefer, learners will feel that you don't value their views. Over-editing is also a good way to lose neutrality. The first rule of recording is, therefore, to be sure to capture the key words that people use when expressing their ideas.

Having said that, facilitators are constantly challenged to create short, concise summaries of lengthy thoughts. Here are two simple rules to follow when recording group discussions:

**Rule #1- Use their words.** Listen carefully for the key words used and ensure that those words show up on the flip chart. Reinforce this by saying things like:

> *"I'm writing the word 'disaster' because you emphasized it."*
> *"Let me read back what I wrote to make sure I've accurately captured your point."*

**Rule #2 – Ask permission to change words.** When people ramble, or can't find the right words, offer wording, but get approval for your edits to ensure that what's recorded reflects what the person intended to say. Say something like:

> *"I've shortened what you said to . . . Is that okay?"*
> *"Can I use the word…?"*
> *"Is it okay to record that idea this way?"*

# Final Recording Tip

A great technique to keep up your sleeve is to invite speakers to dictate the exact words they want to see recorded. This is useful if you can't figure out what the student is saying or if you momentarily lose focus. In these situations, say something like:

*"Tell me what you want me to write."*
*"Give me the exact words you need to see on the board."*

## Recording Do's and Don'ts

**DO**

Do write down exactly what learners say. If comments have to be edited, always use their key words. Check to make sure that what is written captures the meaning expressed.

Do use verbs and make phrases fairly complete. For example, recording "work group" is not as helpful as "work group to meet Mondays at 10 a.m." Always be sure the notes make sense, even to someone who wasn't at the meeting.

Do talk and write at the same time. This is necessary in order to maintain a good pace. Practiced facilitators can write one thing while asking the next question.

Do move around and act alive. There is nothing worse than a facilitator who seems to be chained to the flip chart. If an important point is being made, walk closer to the person who's talking so you can better pay attention.

Do write in black, blue or some other dark color. Use fairly large letters so it can be read from the back of the room.

Do post flip chart sheets around the room so that people can keep track of what has been discussed.

**DON'T**

Don't write down your personal interpretation of things. These are their notes. If unsure, ask, *"What should I write down?"*

Don't worry about handwriting. If you make a fuss, it will inhibit others from getting up and taking a turn at facilitating.

Don't hide behind the flip chart or talk to it. Unless you're writing, stand squarely beside it, facing the members when reading back notes.

Don't stand passively at the flip chart while a long discussion is going on without writing anything down. Ideas don't need to be in complete sentences before recording them. Make note of key words and ideas. Comprehensive statements can be formulated later.

Don't use red or pale pastels that are impossible to see from a distance.

Don't cover the notes already made so that no one can reference the points already made.

*Facilitating in the Classroom*

## Starting a Facilitation

Whenever you step into the facilitator role, create clarity by using something called a *Start Sequence*. *Start Sequences* have the following three components:

| The Start Sequence |
|---|
| **1. The Purpose** – Facilitators always start by making a statement that clearly describes the goal of the facilitated discussion. This is <u>what</u> will be discussed. This can take the form of a simple goal statement, or it can be more detailed and include a description of the desired outcomes.<br><br>**2. The Process** – Facilitators tell group members <u>how</u> the session will be conducted. This helps the participants understand how decisions will be made, the speaking order, and any structuring tools that will be used. The process description should also clarify if members are making the final decision or if they're simply being asked for input regarding a decision that will be made later by others.<br><br>**The Timeframe** – Facilitators tell people how long the entire discussion will take. In more complex conversations, timeframes should also be provided for each segment within the discussion. |

### *Start Sequence* Example

The sample below shows how simple and helpful *Start Sequences* are for keeping learning activities focused.

> **Purpose:** We're now going to share the data that you collected during your research.
>
> **Process**: A spokesperson from each research team will present their results. Please hold all questions until the end of each presentation.
>
> **Timeframe**: Each team will have ten minutes to present, with an additional five minutes at the end for Q & A, for a total of 15 minutes per team.

When you're planning a lengthy exercise, always write the *Start Sequence* on a flip chart or whiteboard for all to see.

*Chapter Two: Facilitation Core Practices*

## During a Facilitation

Once an activity is underway, it can easily get stuck or go off track, even when there's a clear *Start Sequence* in place. This can happen because:

- the topic may be more complex than was anticipated
- the original timeframes may not have been realistic
- a few people may be talking too much
- the learners have become tired or lost focus
- no one in the group is managing time

Sometimes there are obvious signs that the activity isn't working, but there are also times when a breakdown is harder to detect. That's why it's important to periodically stop the action and conduct what's known as a *Process Check*.

## What is a Process Check?

A *Process Check* is simply stopping the action to ask how it's going. Think of this as taking the pulse.

**1. Check for progress:** Ask the students if the purpose is still clear? Do they think that the activity is still on track? Are they making progress?

When to check for progress: If groups look stuck, when the conversation goes in circles, when people look confused, or at periodic intervals.

**2. Check the process:** Ask students if they feel that the tool or approach being used is working. Ask how much longer they're willing to keep using a tool or approach that isn't working. Offer other tools if they want to switch methods.

When to check the process: When the tool being used isn't yielding results, or isn't being applied properly, or at periodic intervals.

**3. Check the pace**: Ask students if things are moving at the right pace. Are they moving too slowly and getting behind? Are they rushing through?

When to check the pace: When timelines are not being met, or at periodic intervals.

**4. Check the people**: Ask people how they're feeling. Ask if anyone feels frustrated, bored, tired, confused, etc.

When to check the people: When the activity has been going on for a long time, when people are silent and or look withdrawn, when people yawn or look frustrated.

*Facilitating in the Classroom*

| **The 4 P's of *Process Checking*** |
|---|
| There are four basic areas of inquiry in *Process Checking*:<br><br>    1. Progress<br>    2. Process<br>    3. Pace<br>    4. People |

## Staying on Track

It's easy for group discussions to get sidetracked. Someone might ask a question that's best answered later, or learners might start a discussion that isn't part of the current topic. When this happens in a meeting, group facilitators place the off-track item into something called a *Parking Lot.*

A *Parking Lot* is simply a blank sheet of paper posted on a side wall or a designated portion of a whiteboard. Whenever someone introduces an element that has the potential to either sidetrack or preempt the learning activity, it gets recorded on that sheet.

Here are a few tips about how to park an off-topic question or comment:

- acknowledge the item by paraphrasing its key points
- invite the student to elaborate some more
- write the idea or question on the *Parking Lot* sheet or space
- inform the class that this could be important but needs to be addressed later
- thank the student who raised the point

Placing an item into a *Parking Lot* creates an obligation to check on it later. Sometimes these questions answer themselves. In other cases, they'll need to be discussed or forwarded to a future class.

Reviewing parked items at the end of a class enables you to check in with people about whether or not their questions have been answered. Engaging the whole class in addressing *Parking Lot* items can be a great way to end a class.

*Chapter Two: Facilitation Core Practices*

## Ending a Facilitation

At the end of every discussion, facilitative teachers either provide a summary of key points or ask learners to offer a summary. This brings closure to the session and ensures that everyone is clear about what was learned.

While most classroom discussions do not involve making decisions, there will be times when the class might be involved in reaching a joint conclusion about their research or deliberations. Here is how decision making changes the end of a facilitated discussion.

---

**Ending a Non-Decision-Making Discussion:**

At the end of a discussion during which students shared information, brainstormed ideas, or made lists, it's a facilitator best practice to provide a summary of the points discussed. This allows people to add any points that were missed and it brings closure.

**Ending a Decision-Making Discussion:**

At the end of a session during which group members made one or more decisions, facilitators recap what was decided to ratify the outcome, and ensure that everybody is on the same page. This can include:

- reviewing the details of the decision
- checking the decision for clarity and completeness
- ratifying the decision by asking if everyone can live with the outcome
- identifying next steps and creating detailed action plans

---

In addition to bringing closure to discussions, facilitators also do some or all of the following:

- check in on *Parking Lot* items to make sure all of them have been addressed
- ensure everyone leaves with clarity about what was learned
- allow learners to take digital snapshots of notes they need
- help members evaluate the session
- thank everyone for their active participation

## Facilitating Online Learning

More and more classes are being taught online these days. Right now, this is most common at the college level, where 30% to 50% of classes are being taught this way. It's very likely that this trend will spread to lower grades.

Online courses are typically taught entirely online. Content is formatted using online learning software, such as *Articulate, Lectora,* and *Adapt.* Students view the material, complete posted assignments, and take tests entirely online, without interacting with the instructor who created the course.

There are also several hybrid approaches to online learning such as:

- The teacher posts a pre-recorded lecture on the school share site. Learners view the lecture individually. They subsequently come to the classroom to discuss the topic, or conduct experiments and exercises related to the online lecture.

- The teacher delivers a lecture in the classroom. Learners then join online groups to discuss the content.

- The teacher remotely conducts a class with learners using software such as *Skype* or *Zoom.* The teacher presents material and facilitates a discussion using the core practices previously described in this book.

While facilitation was originally designed for face-to-face interaction, the core practices work even when learners aren't all in the same place.

If a group of learners are supposed to meet on their own, the facilitative teacher provides either a detailed discussion guide or observation sheet to ensure that a structured approach will be used. Below are two examples of how a teacher can provide facilitation support even when they aren't present.

- **Example # 1: Presentation skills.** Students go online to view a presentation that the teachers have pre-selected as an example of an excellent presentation technique. This might be a highly rated *TEDTalk* or a *YouTube* video by a famous world leader.

- Before they view the video, students download an observation sheet that lists the best practices of great presentations. This sheet offers criteria such as: connects with the audience, tells a compelling story, uses humor, has a clear beginning, middle and end, has a clear focus or message, uses a dynamic delivery, shares an inspirational message, conveys authenticity, maintains consistent high energy, and so forth.

- Students use the structured observation sheet to assess the presentations. They summarize their insights and then create a short presentation. Each student in the group records their summary on the school share-site.

- Other students in the online study group are assigned the task of reviewing one or more of their classmates' videos using the original structured observation sheet. Through the school share-site they offer each other written suggestions about how they can further improve their presentation skills.

- **Example # 2 – Literature class.** On the school share site, the teachers post a structured reading guide, which lists some of the things to look for when critiquing a work of fiction. These elements might include things like: how the characters are developed, how suspense is created, how the plot is moved forward, how time is managed, the role of the narrator, and so forth. Students download this guide and use it to make notes as they read the book.

- Small discussion groups of four to five students chat online to share their observations about the book. Each student writes a short essay about the book or creates a short video that summarizes their assessment of the key features of the work. Essays or videos are posted on the school share-site.

In each of these above examples, the teacher facilitated by providing detailed discussion guides or criteria. These tools provided structure to the activity. While this is not facilitation in the classic sense, it none-the-less fulfills the key role of the facilitator, which is to provide structure that enables organized, engaged learning.

*Facilitating in the Classroom*

## The Best and Worst Practices of Facilitative Teachers

### Some of the best facilitator practices to adopt:

- Create an open and trusting atmosphere.
- Provide a clear structure for all activities.
- Help people understand what's in if for them.
- Listen actively to fully understand what's being said.
- Work hard to stay neutral while in facilitator mode.
- Ask questions to encourage participation and conversation.
- Speak in simple and direct language.
- Display energy and appropriate levels of assertiveness.
- Stay open to ideas you don't personally favor.
- Provide decision-making tools when needed.
- Stay flexible and ready to change direction, if necessary.
- Clearly state the purpose, process, and timeframe for each discussion.
- Periodically check with students to determine if it's working.
- Make notes that reflect what participants mean.
- Make sure every session ends with a clear summary.
- Ensure that students feel connected to what they learned.

### Some of the worst facilitator pitfalls to avoid:

- Fail to provide a clear structure for activities.
- Remain oblivious to student ideas or needs.
- Fail to listen carefully to what's being said.
- Lose track of key ideas.
- Take poor notes or change the meaning of what's said.
- Provide content that pre-empts learner discovery and reflection.
- Get defensive.
- Dismiss ideas.
- Avoid or ignore conflict.
- Fail to keep track of time.
- Let a few students dominate.
- Never check how the class is going.
- Fail to provide decision-making methods.
- Be overly passive about the process.
- Have no alternate approaches in mind.
- Let discussions get sidetracked.
- Let discussions end without proper closure.
- Be oblivious about when to stop.

# Facilitation at a Glance Cue Card

**To Start a Facilitation**
- Explain your role
- Clarify the purpose of the session
- Explain the process
- Set time frames
- Create a *Parking Lot*
- Establish *Norms*
- Start the discussion

**Core Practices**
- Explain the process
- Stay neutral
- Listen actively
- Ask questions
- Paraphrase
- Record ideas
- Synthesize ideas
- Stay on track
- Test assumptions
- Provide summaries

**During A Facilitation**
- Check the purpose
- Check the process
- Check the pace
- Check the people
- Park off topic items
- Intervene if things go off the rails

**Conflict Management**
- Revisit *Norms*
- Vent feelings
- Surface concerns
- Solve problems
- Redirect behaviors
- Solicit feedback

**To End a Facilitation**
- Summarize discussions
- Help groups make decisions
- Round up parked items
- Help learners summarize what they learned
- Evaluate the learning activity

**Structured Conversation**
- Sequential Questioning
- *Forcefield* Analysis
- *Brainstorming*
- Constructive Controversy
- Gap Analysis
- Decision Grids
- Systematic Problem Solving

*Facilitating in the Classroom*

# Chapter Three: Effective Questioning

Questions are the heart and soul of facilitation. That's because questions are the main tool for encouraging learners to reflect, imagine, buy-in, identify problems, and discover solutions. To explore questioning, chapter three will:

- describe the principles of effective questioning
- review question types
- label various question formats
- explain the importance of follow-on questions
- define how facilitative teachers respond to questions
- examine a tool called *The Five Why's*
- provide sample questions
- describe key questioning do's and don'ts

## The Principles of Effective Questioning

One of the great challenges of questioning effectively is that there isn't a standard set of questions that works for every situation. A line of questioning that works really well for one subject area will not be relevant in another. Even the sample questions in this chapter are only offered as food for thought. It's always important to remember that every question should be carefully evaluated to ensure that it's appropriate. The following guidelines can help:

1. **Customize for context:** Be sure that questions are sensitive to things like the age of the learners, the stresses facing them at school or at home, and the level of their previous exposure to the topic.

2. **Create inviting questions:** Avoid embedding too many of your own thoughts and suggestions inside questions. This can lead learners to give answers that they think you will like. This can make your questioning feel manipulative. Ask the kind of open-ended questions that encourage deep, creative thought.

3. **Ask with sensitivity:** Unless you decide to deliberately confront learners to shake them out of complacent thinking, questions should always be asked mindfully. That means avoiding asking questions that could make a learner feel that they are being called out in front of their peers.

4. **Clarify assumptions:** Check out your understanding of what students are saying. Sometimes they use language differently or understate how they really feel. Ask things like: *"Am I correct in thinking that...?" "Let me see if I've understood correctly that..."* or *"Are you saying that...?"*

## Question Types

There are two basic question types: closed-ended and open-ended. Each type has its uses. However, facilitators predominantly use open-ended questions because they encourage people to really think.

| Type of Question | Description | Examples |
| --- | --- | --- |
| **Closed-ended** | Elicits one-word answers and tends to close discussion. | *"Does everyone understand the changes we've discussed?"* |
| | Solicits yes/no answers or ratings. | *"Where is this on a scale of 1 to 5, with 5 being excellent?"* |
| | Useful to clarify and test assumptions. | *"Have I given a clear description of the situation?"* |
| | Often begins with *"is,"* *"can,"* *"how many,"* or *"does"* | *"Does any of this need more elaboration?"* |
| | | *"Is there anything else that we need to add before we move along?"* |
| **Open-ended** | Requires more than yes/no answers. | *"What ideas do you have for explaining the sudden shift in military tactics in the middle of the western campaign?"* |
| | Stimulates thinking. Often begins with or contains *"What,"* *"How,"* *"When,"* or *"Why"*. | *"If we were going to do something totally innovative, what would that look like?"* |

*Facilitating in the Classroom*

## Question Formats

The questions in this chapter are organized according to their intention and represent different questioning formats. Professional facilitators use various formats to avoid getting into the rut of asking only one type of question.

**Fact-finding questions** are targeted at verifiable data such as who, what, when, where, and how much. Use them to gather information about the current situation.

> *"Why did the Black Death move through Europe so quickly?"*
> *"What did people do to make matters worse?"*

**Feeling-finding questions** ask for subjective information that gets at the participants' opinions, feelings, values, and beliefs.

> *"How do you think people felt as the plague intensified?"*
> *"Which emotions are helpful in catastrophes? Which are not?"*

**Tell-me-more questions** encourage people to provide more detail.

> *"Can you say more about that? What else comes to mind?"*
> *"What do you think caused that to happen?"*

**Best/worst questions** help you understand potential opportunities in the present situation. They let you probe at both ends of the spectrum.

> *"What were the best things that people did in reaction to the plague?"*
> *"What were the worst things that people did in reaction to the plague?"*

**Third-party questions** help uncover thoughts in an indirect manner by allowing people to speculate on what others might think without challenging them to reveal their personal thoughts.

> *"Why did some people feel that the plague was just retribution?"*
> *"Why did other people argue against that idea?"*

**Magic-wand questions** help you explore people's desires. Also known as crystal ball questions, these are useful to temporarily remove obstacles.

> *"If you had been in total control and had endless resources, what would you have done to manage the plague?"*

*Chapter Three: Effective Questioning*

## The Importance of Follow-on Questions

One of the most important aspects of effective questioning is the ability to ask the right follow-on questions. Follow-on questioning matters because the initial response to a question often fails to go deep enough. Think of follow-on questioning as *peeling the onion* in order to get to the heart of the matter. Some lines of questioning may even need to be pursued three or four times to get to the real core of an issue or topic.

While the exact wording of follow-on questions can't be predicted, here are some general principles to keep in mind:

1. Start with straightforward fact-finding questions.
2. Follow up with questions that clarify the initial responses.
3. Ask for the rationale behind those responses.
4. Ask how things unfolded.
5. Use feeling-finding questions to get at the core of the matter.
6. Use third-party or magic-wand questions to encourage out-of-the-box thinking.

## Responding to Questions

Facilitative teachers react differently to content questions than do traditional instructors. Instead of immediately providing answers, they bounce the question back to the students to encourage them to think more deeply. Here are some examples of how that looks. Facilitative teachers do however, answer process questions to clear up confusion about how an activity is being conducted. Here are some examples of how that looks.

**Scenario 1: During an activity or group discussion, a student asks a process question about how the activity is supposed to unfold.**

**In Instructor mode:** The teacher answers the question.
**In facilitator mode:** The teacher answers the question to immediately clear up any confusion about the steps in the process or the timing.

**Scenario 2: During an activity or group discussion, a student asks a content question.**

**In instructor mode:** The teacher answers the question.

**In facilitator mode:** The teacher repeats the question then asks the student for more information. The teacher then asks if anyone else has an interest in that question, or has anything to add to the question. The facilitative teacher doesn't answer the question, but instead places it in the *Parking Lot*. The teacher then asks everyone to be on the lookout for the answer during the upcoming activity. At the end of the class, the teacher goes back to the *Parking Lot* to find out how many of the parked questions have been answered. The teacher only adds content for those that remain unanswered.

*Facilitating in the Classroom*

**Scenario 3: A student asks a really great content question.**

<u>In instructor mode:</u> The teacher answers the question.

<u>In facilitator mode:</u> The teacher paraphrases the question, then says, *"Let's all think about this for a minute. How would you answer it?"* This creates conversation that brings in different perspectives. The teacher only adds missed facts at the end of the group discussion.

When you deliberately avoid answering content questions, it encourages students to dig deeper and share views with other students.

## Question Cascades

One of the most effective ways to use questioning is to drill down more deeply into student responses. In the traditional classroom, teachers ask students to report on what they learned. In the experiential classroom, teachers delve into how an answer was formulated. This helps learners to hone their critical thinking skills.

Below is an example of a question cascade to engage students in delving more deeply into how they did their work.

- *"What assumptions did you make at the outset?"*
- *"Did you break the question or problem into parts? Name those parts."*
- *"Did you define or set limits for the scope of the question/problem/equation?"*
- *"Did you have a strategy for working on the question/problem/equation?"*
- *"What's your answer to the question/problem/equation?"*
- *"How did you reach that conclusion?"*
- *"How confident are you in your answer?"*
- *"Can you reword your response/answer in simpler terms?"*
- *"Have we ever encountered a question/problem/equation like this before?" "What ideas have we previously explored that were helpful?"*
- *"How did you check your steps or your answer?"*
- *"What correct or incorrect assumptions did you make along the way?"*
- *"What pitfalls or dead ends did you run into?"*
- *"Is there anything you overlooked?"*
- *"Explain your approach to someone who missed the class.*
- *"How would you convince someone that your answer is the right one if they arrived at a different solution/conclusion?"*
- *"Can you create a chart or draw a picture to explain your answer?"*
- *"Is there another way to approach this question/problem/equation?"*
- *"What have you learned that could apply to other challenges?"*
- *"How can we connect what was learned from this activity to other topics or to the outside world?"*

## *The 5 Whys*

No exploration of questioning would be complete without mentioning something known as *The 5 Whys.* This technique consists of asking why over and over again to prompt people to drill down to root causes.

Its greatest use is when someone gives a reason for something that sounds more like a symptom or surface manifestation. Try using it the next time students come to you with a problem that they want you to solve. Instead of fixing it for them, facilitate them through *The 5 Whys* so that they discover the solution for themselves.

**How to do *The 5 Why's***

**Step #1:** Clarify the symptom
**Step #2:** Ask: *"Why is this happening?"* paraphrase the response
**Step #3:** Ask: *"Why is this happening?"* about the last response
**Step #4:** Repeat three more times, each time paraphrasing all comments
**Step # 5:** Stop to review the analysis. Ask if the root-cause has been discovered.

**A *5 Whys* Example**: Our science team's robot won't start. (symptom)

1st Why  - What's going on? (The battery's dead.)
2nd Why - What other parts aren't working? (The alternator isn't functioning.)
3rd Why  - Why isn't the alternator working? (The alternator belt is broken.)
4th Why  - Why did it break? (The belt is worn out and has never been replaced.)
5th Why  - Why wasn't it ever replaced? (We didn't create a repair schedule.)

*The 5 Why's* example above, illustrates how useful facilitation is outside the classroom. When a student approaches with a problem you can either solve it for them or facilitate them through a set of steps that help them solve it for themselves.

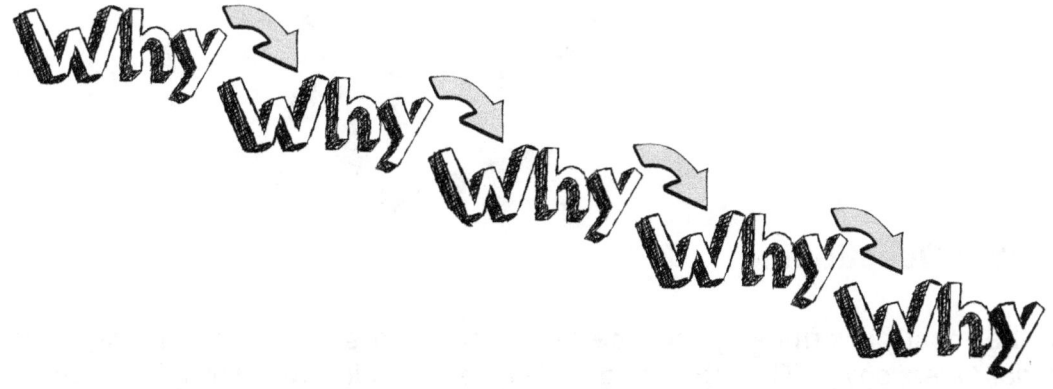

*Facilitating in the Classroom*

## Structured Observation Sheets

It's important to note that the effective use of questions doesn't always involve asking questions in the classroom. Facilitative teachers often create a set of questions in advance of a class. Then they hand these out to guide group deliberations.

This has a number of distinct advantages. First, it allows you to provide structure to online classes without being present. This application is described in additional detail on page 39. Second, creating structured questionnaires or observation sheets enables you to give each small group in your classroom a different focus for their explorations.

Let's look at an example in an art appreciation class:

- In advance of the lesson, identify the key traits you want students to observe. Provide a simple sentence to describe each trait. This can be things like balance, composition, use of light, how the artist moves the eye, mastery of the material, level of complexity, what's being communicated, etc.
- If small groups are each assessing a different work, give all of the groups the same sheet. If small groups are all assessing the same work, consider giving each group an observation sheet that focuses on just a few of the traits.
- If you use the latter approach, create new groups made up of people who looked at different elements of the work. Ask groups to share their separate observations to come up with an assessment of the artwork being studied.

Structured observation sheets are especially important for online chat sessions. These give students key points to discuss as they share their conclusions about a topic.

## Sequential Questioning

One of the most powerful ways to use questions is to structure an activity known as *Sequential Questioning*. This hour-long activity is engaging and thought provoking. It's perfect at the end of a subject to challenge learners to summarize what they've learned. It's also a lot of fun. Read the full description on page 112 and give it a try.

*Chapter Three: Effective Questioning*

# The Question Bank

On the following pages you'll find examples that will help you formulate great probing questions. The best way to view these samples is to see them as food for thought. While some of these sample questions can be used off the shelf, they'll always be more effective if they're adapted to fit the context. Also be aware that some of these questions may only be relevant to more mature students.

Note that these questions don't always need to be asked in front of the class. They can be posed to pairs or small groups or even asked in written form.

## Questions that Help Students Get to Know One Another

- *"Tell us one interesting thing about where you grew up."*
- *"Tell us about the most awesome thing that has ever happened to you."*
- *"Complete this sentence: My dream summer job is ...?"*
- *"What's your hidden talent?"*
- *"What do you love to do when you aren't in school?"*
- *"If you had to condense your life story into two sentences, what would they be?"*
- *"If you had to name one skill you'd like to acquire, what would it be?"*
- *"What unique gift, experience, or skill do you bring to this class/project?"*
- *"What would other students say is your main talent or best trait?"*
- *"What always motivates you to do a great job?"*
- *"What trait would you most like to see in a fellow team member/classmate?"*

## Questions to Create Buy-in

- *"What one or two things would you most like to gain from this class?"*
- *"What's the burning question that you need to have answered by this class?"*
- *"Describe the most positive thing you could personally gain from this project."*
- *"How will understanding this topic help you with other subjects/in life?"*

## Questions to Establish Behavioral *Norms* or Rules of Conduct

- *"Think back to a time when you were on a team where everybody got along. What attitudes and behaviors did people exhibit? What rules did they follow?"*
- *"What have you learned is important while working on other projects or teams? Which of these things should this team consider implementing?"*
- *"Describe the best things about being part of a great team? How can we make sure that each of these happens with this team?*
- *"What's the best way to head off or avoid arguments?"*
- *"What's the best way to respond to a point that you don't agree with?"*
- *"What should the rule be about people keeping their commitments?"*
- *"What's the rule about checking messages or using phones during a class?"*

## Questions to Uncover Issues or Problems

- *"How would you describe this problem to an outsider?"*
- *"What's taking place? What are the signs and symptoms?"*
- *"What's causing each of the symptoms that we see?"*
- *"What other problems does this particular problem cause?"*
- *"Who's affected? How are they impacted?"*
- *"Who or what is contributing to the problem?"*
- *"What's been tried in the past and failed?"*
- *"What stops this problem from being solved?"*
- *Keep asking: "Why? Why? Why? Why? Why?"*

## Questions to Encourage Creative Thinking

- *"What would you do if money were no object?"*
- *"What would an eight-year old child suggest? What would an eighty-year old person suggest?"*
- *"If we think revolution instead of evolution, would we do things differently?"*
- *"Think about a group of people who are really creative and successful with their projects. What makes them so innovative?"*
- *"Describe some of the most innovative or creative products and services you have ever heard of or used. What makes them stand out?"*
- *"What's the most obvious solution? What's the least obvious?"*
- *"What's never been done before that we could try?"*

## Questions to Identify Implications

- *"Let's look at the main ideas we've got so far. What are the specific impacts of each suggestion?"*
- *"If we implement the ideas we have so far, what are the unanticipated consequences we might encounter?"*
- *"Look into a crystal ball and tell me about the kinds of unexpected outcomes that we could be creating with the approach we're taking?"*
- *"What's one thing we know for sure about the bottom line on this matter?"*

## Questions to Prompt for Clarity

- *"Please be more specific."*
- *"Say more about that."*
- *"Give us another example."*
- *"Can you say that another way?"*
- *"What's the opposite of that?"*
- *"Someone restate that idea to see if we all understand it the same way."*
- *"Tell us more. How does this impact this topic?"*

*Chapter Three: Effective Questioning*

## Questions to Gain Perspective

- *"Has anyone experienced a similar situation?"*
- *"What assumptions are we making about this idea?"*
- *"What are the pros and cons of this idea?"*
- *"Is this the same old thinking? What would be a new way of seeing this same issue?"*
- *"If we've missed seeing an important dimension of this, what would it be?"*
- *"How might others see this issue?"*
- *"Does anyone have something totally different to suggest?"*

## Questions to Challenge and Confront

- *"Isn't what you're suggesting, exactly what was done before?"*
- *"Why do you think your project hasn't been as bold as it needs to be?"*
- *"If there's one major thing that's holding this effort back, what is it?"*
- *"What do you think we could do to take things to the next level?"*

The final question to ask when you sense that there's still something that hasn't been brought to the surface is:

*"What's the one question we haven't asked ourselves yet?"*

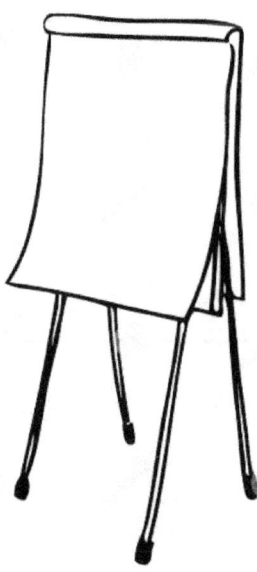

*Facilitating in the Classroom*

## Questioning Do's and Don'ts

| **DO's** | **DON'Ts** |
|---|---|
| Do ask clear, concise questions covering a single issue. | Don't ask rambling, ambiguous questions that cover multiple issues. |
| Do ask a good combination of questions. | Don't get stuck asking only fact-finding questions. |
| Do retool questions to fit the context. | Don't ask everyone the same question. |
| Do ask challenging questions that stimulate thought. | Don't ask questions without providing an opportunity for thought. |
| Do use mostly open-ended questions. | Don't forget that closed-ended questions can be useful for testing understanding. |
| Do ask questions that are sensitive to feelings. | Don't ask trick questions designed to entrap or fool people. |
| Do ask reasonable questions based on what people know. | Don't ask questions that most people can't answer. |
| Do ask honest and relevant questions. | Don't ask questions that lead students to the answer you want. |
| Do ask appropriate follow-on questions that get to the heart of the matter. | Don't assume that the first answer a student offers is the only facet of the issue. |

# Chapter Four: Decision Making in the Classroom

Experiential learning involves frequent use of group decision-making tools. These tools add value by creating engagement. This chapter will:

- describe the difference between decision-making and non-decision-making conversations
- compare five core decision-making methods
- describe alternative ways of using *Multi-voting*

## The Need to Make Group Decisions

With experiential learning it's essential to provide learners with methods that help the whole class to make a joint decision. Group decision making will be needed to:

- identify which topics or options to explore
- rank the importance of factors in a situation
- decide the outcome of a debate or exercise
- take the pulse of the group
- evaluate a presentation or project

Over the years, facilitators have developed methods for engaging groups in decision making. Before we address those methods, it's important to know that there are two types of conversations: those in which ideas are merely being shared versus those in which decisions are being made. Understanding this difference is key, because these two types of conversations are facilitated differently.

## Non-Decision-Making Conversations

Non-decision-making conversations are those in which students simply share thoughts or information. During non-decision-making discussions, the facilitative teacher quickly records ideas without checking to see if anyone else agrees. Some examples of non-decision-making conversations include:

- a *Brainstorming* session in which all ideas are accepted and not judged
- an information-sharing session in which students share their personal knowledge or update each other
- a relationship-building session in which learners get to know each other
- a discussion aimed at making a list of individual preferences or key factors in a situation

In non-decision-making conversations, all ideas are recorded without being filtered. Sometimes, these ideas are ranked and sorted later using one of the *Multi-voting* techniques described on the following pages. The role of the facilitator in non-decision-making conversations is to simply paraphrase, clarify, and record.

*Facilitating in the Classroom*

## Decision-Making Conversations

Decision-making conversations are those discussions in which student ideas are combined to create a statement that everyone can live with. These statements typically describe either an action plan or a rule. Some examples of decision-making discussions include:

- a discussion to create a set of classroom rules that everyone agrees to honor
- a discussion to merge a number of options into a single plan that the entire group supports
- a discussion to sort through a series of ideas to identify a solution to a problem that works for everyone

Facilitators manage decision-making conversations by paraphrasing to clarify ideas. They then bounce those ideas around the room so that others can add their perspectives. When all ideas have been collected, the facilitator makes a statement that summarizes everything that was said into a single decision statement. The facilitator then checks in with each person to make sure that they can live with the final decision.

Leading these types of decision-making conversations is difficult and only works in small groups of ten or less. To make decisions in a larger group, use the following two steps: conduct a non-decision-making discussion to generate a list of options, then use one of the *Multi-voting* techniques described on page 59.

## Conversation Types Summary

| Non-Decision-Making | Decision-Making |
| --- | --- |
| listen to an idea | listen to an idea |
| paraphrase to clarify | paraphrase to clarify |
| ask for more info | get others to comment |
| summarize ideas | combine ideas |
| record ideas | summarize |
| read summary | check for consent/*Multi-vote* |
|  | ratify the decision |

*Chapter Four: Decision-Making in the Classroom*

## Decision-Making Options

Experiential learning activities often require the use of decision-making tools

> Here are the five ways to make a group decision:
>
> 1. *Win/Win Compromise*
> 2. *Consensus Building*
> 3. *One person decides*
> 4. *Majority Voting*
> 5. *Multi-voting*

### 1. Win/Win Compromise

If the class is faced with the need to decide between two alternate approaches, you could simply help them to choose one option or the other. Unfortunately, this will result in winners and losers. Also, each of the competing alternatives may have valuable elements. Instead, help the class identify the strong points of the two options. Then help them construct a middle position that includes the best features from each of the two competing ideas. This takes more time than a simple up or down majority vote, but allows you to build a win/win approach.

**Goal:** To construct a middle position between two competing ideas.

**Tools:** Three pieces of flip chart paper or three sections of a whiteboard, plus markers or voting dots.

**Steps**: Post three sheets of flip chart paper on a bare wall or create three sections on a whiteboard. From left to right, label each of the three sections: #1 Option A , #2 Our Approach, and #3 Option B. Draw a line down the middle of the sheet marked Option A and also down the middle of the sheet marked Option B. The divided pages are the format for a Pros & Cons exercise. In this case, use Strengths and Weaknesses.

*Facilitating in the Classroom*

Start with Option A. Invite learners to describe this option in detail. Then have them tell you all the best features of Option A. Write these in the Strengths column. Facilitate this *Brainstorming* discussion until you have a complete list of the strengths of Option A. Then do the same thing for Option B.

Go back to the flip chart sheet for Option A to facilitate a discussion of all its weaknesses. Record all comments. Facilitate the same discussion for Option B. When this is done, read back all of the pros and cons of both options and check that this assessment is complete.

Hand out voting dots or markers. Inform students of the number of times they'll be able to vote. (To rank items, allow approximately half the number of votes, as there are items. For example, to rank 10 items, allow five votes.) Remind learners that they may not vote more than once for a single item.

Invite students to mill around to post their votes. Remind them to select only the most important features in the strengths column for both options. Tally the votes to identify the highest ranked items. Read this summary aloud to the class.

Go to the middle flip chart and facilitate a discussion that challenges the students to identify a way forward that incorporates the top ranked items on both strength lists.
If you have a large class, divide students into triads. Give the trios ten minutes to come up with ways to combine the most important strengths from each option.

Collect student ideas and write bullet-point summaries of the suggestions on the middle board. Keep tweaking the wording of this new middle position until you sense agreement. Challenge anyone who's not in agreement with parts of the middle position to suggest amendments. Keep editing and refining the points that make up the middle position until you have something that everyone can live with. End with a summary of the joint plan.

## 2. Consensus Building

If the class needs to make an extremely important decision about a topic that impacts everyone, take the time to create a solution that incorporates input from all parties.

Consensus building is different from other decision-making approaches because it starts with the problem or issue, instead of with a solution. This takes time, but leaves people feeling that they can live with the result because they contributed to each part of the process.

**Goal:** To create a decision that everyone can live with.

**Tools:** Flip chart or whiteboard, markers, voting dots or tiny sticky notes.

**Steps:** Ensure that everyone has a clear understanding of the situation or issue to be decided. Facilitate a discussion in which you invite everyone to tell you the story of the current situation. Record all of the known facts. This creates a shared understanding of the problem or challenge.

Facilitate a discussion to generate a list of potential courses of action or solutions. This is a *Brainstorming* session during which you accept all ideas, even if they're impractical or contradictory. Just let the ideas flow.

Use one of the *Multi-voting* approaches describe later in this chapter to sort the ideas. Tally the votes. Write the highest ranked ideas on a new section of the whiteboard. Combine these suggestions to create an action plan. Read it aloud and ratify the decision with the group.

By analyzing all of the relevant facts together, jointly generating possible solutions and ranking those ideas, you arrive at a solution or set of action steps that everyone feels they had a role in creating. (The *Systematic Problem Solving Model* on page 126 is an example of a consensus building process.)

### 3. One Person Decides

Sometimes the quickest and simplest way to reach a decision is to ask one person to make that decision on behalf of the whole group. This is a good method to use if the issue is relatively trivial or has little impact on the class.

The main drawback of a one-person decision is that it will have extremely low buy-in from the rest of the class. This is okay if the matter is inconsequential, but using this approach to decide something students really care about, will create resistance.

To overcome potential resistance all learners can be invited to provide input to the decision maker before a decision is rendered. As a result, learners will feel that their views have been taken into account.

**Goal:** To find the right person and empower that person to make a decision on behalf of the group.

**Tools:** Flip chart or whiteboard and marker.

**Steps:** Identify the person who's going to make the decision. Clarify the decision they'll be making. If you're concerned with resistance, facilitate a short class discussion to get everyone's views on the matter. Summarize the advice gleaned from the group. Use *Multi-voting* to help students to identify which of their views most need to be considered. Thank everyone for their input and explain that the decision maker will work hard to incorporate their input. Ask for everyone's commitment to support whatever they decide.

*Facilitating in the Classroom*

### 4. Majority voting

This is the simplest and easiest way to make a decision. Just ask for a show of hands, and you have a decision. If the decision is sensitive, you can hand out slips of paper and conduct a majority vote in secret.

The big downside of majority voting is that it creates winners and losers. Some individuals get what they want, while others get nothing. Using a secret ballot to conduct a majority vote will make it feel safer, but will nonetheless create winners and losers.

For this reason reserve majority voting to decide trivial matters like asking a group which warm-up game they want to play, or to decide housekeeping issues. Because it's divisive, avoid using majority voting to make any decision in cases where division on that issue will divide the class.

### 5. *Multi-voting*

Facilitators invented *Multi-voting* to remedy the polarizing effect of *Majority Voting*. In *Multi-voting*, you offer students a range of choices and a method for arriving at a decision. This may seem like an insignificant difference, but it has a major impact on how people feel about the final outcome.

Instead of either winning or losing, everyone gets at least some of what they want. This results in an *"I can live with it"* attitude, which feels more like a consensus. It's important to point out that *Multi-voting* has specific variations. These are described in step-by-step detail on the pages that follow.

---

**Comparing Voting Methods**

*Majority Voting*

I heard the discussions. I knew what I wanted.
I voted. I lost and got nothing. I'm out.

*Multi-voting*

I heard the discussion. I knew what I wanted.
I voted for several items. I got some of what I wanted. I'm still in.

*Chapter Four: Decision-Making in the Classroom*

## *Multi-voting* Variations

*Multi-voting* offers learners a say and gives them a stake in the outcome. Learners like it because it enables them to give their opinion. It also gets them up and moving around. Below are some different versions of this participative technique.

You will need a few supplies so that people can cast their votes. Here are the items mentioned in the following methods: small sticky note pads, scraps of paper and tape, stick-on voting dots (file folder dots sold in office supply stores), and colored markers.

### *Multi-voting* Variation #1 – *Win/Win Majority Voting*

**Scenario:** You need to help the class decide between two important issues or options, but you don't want to use majority voting since it causes division.

**Goal:** To help a class decide between two options without causing winners and losers.

**Tools:** A sheet of flip chart paper (or section of whiteboard), one strip of 10 stick-on voting dots per person (or 10 slips of paper).

**Steps:** Ask everyone to agree that they will support whichever outcome emerges from the *Multi-vote*. Describe each of the two options so that everyone is clear about the two choices. Name one A and the other B. If it's an issue that group members are passionate about, let people take turns extolling the virtues of their favorite option. You could also facilitate a pros and cons review of both options to provide an objective overview of the two choices.

Draw a line down the middle of a flip chart page (or section of whiteboard). Mark one side Option A, and the other one Option B. Tell students to secretly write either the letter A or B on each of their ten dots or slips. They can mark all 10 with one letter or do a mix that reflects how they feel about the two options. (8-2, 6-4, etc.). When all of the dots are marked, tell students to turn their votes face down. Collect all of the votes in a small box or basket. Mix them up. Get a few volunteers to post all the dots or slips as marked. Tally the votes and ratify the winning option with the group.

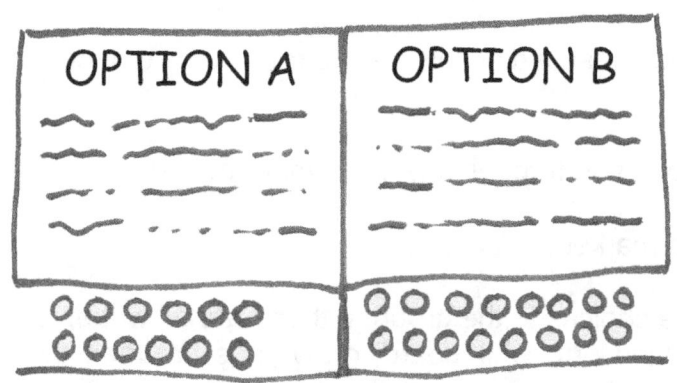

*Facilitating in the Classroom*

### *Multi-voting* Variation #2 - Priority Ranking

**Scenario:** You need to help the class prioritize a long list of possible items, topics, or projects to find out which are of greatest interest.

**Goal**: To help the class rank multiple options.

**Tools:** A strip of four sticky dots or paper slips per person.

**Steps:** Review the items being ranked to ensure that everyone understands all of the choices. Give each person one strip of four sticky dots or four slips of paper. Have them mark each of their dots or slips with one of the following numbers:

These are the values of each dot or slip. Instruct everyone to select the item they feel is most important. This item gets the dot or slip marked 10. Each person's second choice gets the dot or slip marked 7, and so on. Invite people to mill around the flip chart or whiteboard to post their votes. If you want to ensure privacy, number the topics and have people write the topic number on each of their weighted dots. Collect all of the dots and post them. When all of the dots have been posted, ask a volunteer to tally the votes. This method of assigning weights to the dots, results in a clear priority ranking of issues.

Important Note: You can sort up to 20 items with four weighted dots or slips. If you have fewer items than 6, reduce the number of dots or slips to three. In these cases, eliminate the low-ranking dot. Also, don't let anyone place more than one of their dots on a single item. Double voting by individuals skews the results.

### *Multi-voting* Variation #3 – Group Tally

**Scenario:** You need a fast and simple way to rank items that doesn't require voting dots or slips.

**Goal:** To help a group sort through a large number of items.

**Tools:** One colored marker per person.

**Steps:** Describe the choices to the group. If these are all written on a single sheet of flip chart paper, or section of a whiteboard, draw lines between the items so people will know where to place their marks. Let them approach the flip chart or whiteboard to

*Chapter Four: Decision-Making in the Classroom*

place check marks beside all of the items that they favor. This needs to be a forced choice. If there are ten items to choose from, tell people they can only make 5 check marks. If there are eight items, allow only four to be checked off, and so forth. Tally the votes to announce the rankings. As with all *Multi-voting*, do not allow anyone to place more than one check mark on a single item. Double voting skews the outcome.

### *Multi-voting* Variation #4 – Fist of Five

A quick and simple way to gauge the amount of support there is for an idea or suggestion is to invite everyone to show the number of fingers that reflect how they feel.

**Scenario:** You need a fast and simple way to find out how a group feels.

**Goal:** To very quickly take the pulse of the group on a specific subject.

**Tools:** The fingers on one hand.

**Steps:** Clarify the idea or option being decided. Ask if anyone is confused or has a question. On a count of three, ask everyone to flash the fingers of one hand to reflect how they feel about the matter.

> Five fingers – I really like it, let's do it!
> Four fingers – I don't really like it, but I can live with it as it is.
> Three fingers – I can live with it, but it needs one small change.
> Two fingers – I can live with it, but it needs several changes.
> One finger – I'm totally opposed. No way!

If every group member displays either four or five fingers this is considered a consensus. Having everyone show four or five fingers is unlikely though, especially as group size increases. You always need to be ready to explore the reservations behind those who display fewer fingers. When this happens, facilitators invite people to explain their reservations and then challenge them to suggest amendments to the original decision statement so that it will get at least four fingers from everyone.

*Facilitating in the Classroom*

### *Multi-voting* Variation #5 – Sliding Scales

**Scenario:** You want to find out what your students think of a book they read, a video they saw, or a recent activity.

**Goal:** To get a sense of the group sentiment about a topic using a sliding scale.

**Tools:** One single voting dot, paper slip, or marker per person.

**Steps:** Write a short, clear description of the item to be rated on a piece of flip chart paper or section of a whiteboard. Under the description, create a 1 – 5 rating scale.

Describe what each point along the rating scale signifies. Allow a few minutes for people to reflect, then come to the scale to post their rating. If anonymity is important, ask everyone to privately mark their score on a slip of paper. Then have them turn their note face down. Collect the notes in a small box or basket. Ask a volunteer to post all of the ratings. Invite group members to describe the reasons behind the ratings. (Note that there are different descriptors for different situations: from totally ineffective to very effective, from extremely useless to extremely useful, from confusing and incomplete to clear and comprehensive.)

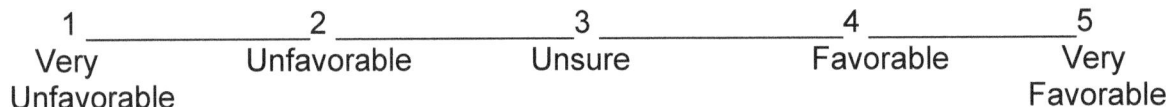

| 1 | 2 | 3 | 4 | 5 |
|---|---|---|---|---|
| Very Unfavorable | Unfavorable | Unsure | Favorable | Very Favorable |

### *Multi-voting* Variation #6 – Color Cards

**Scenario:** You need to get an instant read on how people feel about an issue that's being decided by the group.

**Goal:** To find out how everyone feels about a topic or issue. To surface objections so that they can be addressed.

**Steps:** Give each person five colored cards.

> **Green** – I totally agree!
> **Blue** – I can live with it.
> **Yellow** – I have one or two reservations.
> **Orange** – I have two or more reservations.
> **Red** – I'm totally opposed!

Review the proposal in detail. Check to see if everyone understands what's being decided. Ask students to place all five cards down in their lap. Instruct everyone to pick the card that expresses how they feel about the proposed decision.

Call for a show of cards. Count the cards by color. On a flip chart or whiteboard write down how many students voted in each color group. Invite those who flashed green or blue cards to explain their approval. Ask students who voted yellow or orange to explain their reservations. Write these on a flip chart. Invite those who voted yellow and orange to make suggestions that would get them to change their vote to either green or blue.

When this is done, check in with the students who flashed red cards to see if they've changed their minds. If they haven't, find out why they're still entirely opposed and record those points. Help them look for strategies that move them off red. Record these.

Ask everyone to return their five cards in their lap. For clarification, restate the proposed idea, especially if it's been amended significantly. Repeat the vote to gauge group sentiment. Use this information to decide if you will move forward with the proposal.

### *Multi-voting* Variation #7 – Group Profile

**Scenario:** You want to get everyone out of their seats to take a vote.

**Goal:** To get a visual sense of how everyone feels about a specific topic.

**Tools:** Masking tape.

**Steps:** In an open space, lay down a line of masking tape long enough to accommodate everyone in the room. Place five markers along the line and explain the meaning of each. Clarify the topic being ranked. Invite everyone to get up to stand on the line in the spot that indicates their position in relation to the subject. Only use this method for topics or subjects learners are comfortable revealing where they stand.

Different situations will of course require different key words. On the following page is an example of a group profile line for sorting students on the first day of a whitewater rafting trip. This will help you create balanced teams. Check out the illustration on the next page.

*Facilitating in the Classroom*

| 1 | 2 | 3 | 4 | 5 |
|---|---|---|---|---|
| Very experienced | Did it a few times | Tried it once | Never tried it | Not sure about trying |

### *Multi-voting* Variation #8 – Voting App

**Scenario:** You want to poll the group and you have a tech savvy group in which everyone has a smartphone. Great for really big groups.

**Goal:** To utilize a cell phone app for group decision making.

**Tools:** A smartphone per person and a computer and projector to display results.

**Steps:** Access the app store to find a group voting tool. Current examples include *poleeverywhere.com* and *slido.com*, with new apps being released all the time. Before the class, upload your survey, questionnaire, or list of items to be ranked into the software as per the instructions.

Instruct students to download the app prior to the session. During the session, ask learners to open the app and vote when prompted. The software will tabulate and display the results in graph form on your screen.

This approach offers votes anonymity, which brings their true feelings to the surface. Using a polling app requires set-up time, but can be worth the effort, especially if there's no other practical way to engage the group.

### *Multi-voting* Variation #9 – Group Survey

**Scenario:** You want to conduct a detailed assessment of a class, demonstration, book, or topic in order to gather specific feedback about key elements.

**Goal:** To enable a group to anonymously rate an activity.

**Tools:** Flip chart paper or whiteboard and markers or voting dots.

**Steps:** Create a survey of four to five questions. Write them on a sheet of flip chart paper or section of whiteboard. Under each question draw a 1 – 5 scale.

Invite students to score each question. Give each person a marker and ask them to place an X along the scale under each question, indicating how they feel about that item.

For anonymity, provide colored voting dots or colored slips of paper. Link each color to one of the questions. Allow time for people to privately record their rating on each dot or slip. Collect the dots or slips and post the results on the survey. Share the results and invite students to make suggestions to improve any low ratings.

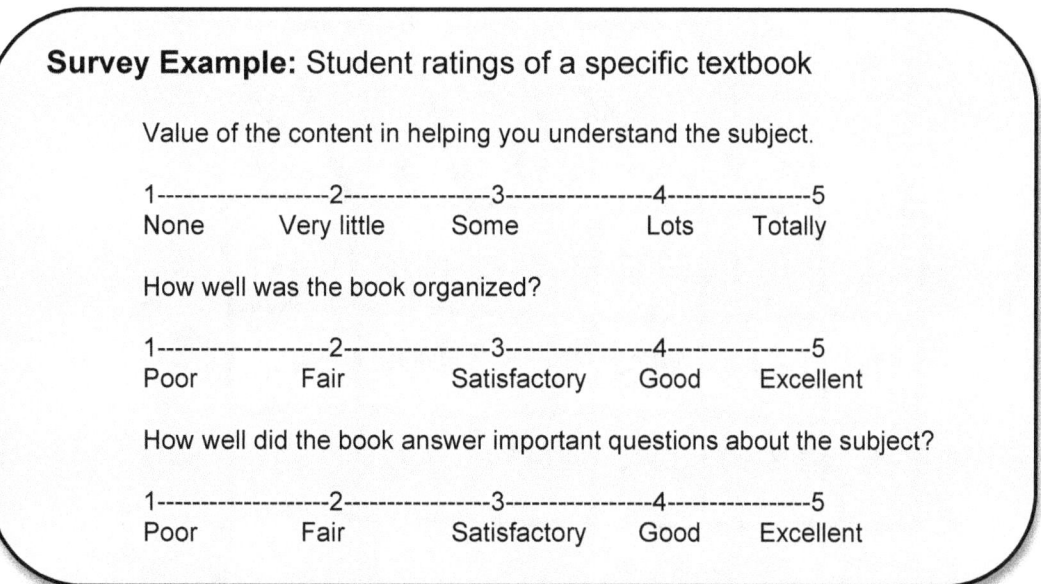

**Survey Example:** Student ratings of a specific textbook

Value of the content in helping you understand the subject.

1--------------------2-----------------3-----------------4----------------5
None    Very little    Some         Lots       Totally

How well was the book organized?

1--------------------2-----------------3-----------------4----------------5
Poor         Fair         Satisfactory      Good      Excellent

How well did the book answer important questions about the subject?

1--------------------2-----------------3-----------------4----------------5
Poor         Fair         Satisfactory      Good      Excellent

### *Multi-voting* Variation #10 – Flash Cards

**Scenario:** You have a large group and you want to get a sense of what they're thinking or feeling. This technique will make a lecture more participative.

**Goal:** To enable students to express their opinions.

**Tools:** A set of cards for each student. You can use a set of three cards: high, medium and low. Another alternative is to have just two cards: either agree or disagree, or true or false. A third option is to create a deck of ten cards with ratings from 1 to 10, with 10 representing the optimal score.

**Steps:** Give each person a set of flash cards. Sprinkle questions throughout your presentation or demonstration. Every time you pose a question, invite students to display their flash cards. Tally the ratings and engage learners in a conversation about how they voted.

Be aware that flash cards with 1 to 10 ratings should never be used to rate the performance of a person or project team. That would be confrontational.

*Facilitating in the Classroom*

## *Multi-voting* Variation #11 – Criteria-based Decision Grid

**Scenario:** You need to help students decide between multiple options that are complex.

**Goal:** To help the group understand how to weigh all of the factors in a situation.

**Tools:** Flip chart or whiteboard and markers.

| OPTION | COST | COMPLEXITY | TIMELINESS | INNOVATION | TOTALS |
|---|---|---|---|---|---|
| A | 1 1 1 1 | 2 3 3 2 | 3 3 3 3 | 4 4 3 4 | 43 |
| B | 1 2 1 1 | 3 4 3 3 | 3 4 3 4 | 4 4 3 3 | 45 |
| C | 1 2 2 1 | 3 3 4 3 | 3 3 4 4 | 3 4 3 3 | 46 |

**Steps:** At the top of the flip chart or whiteboard write a brief description of the options under consideration. Check in with each person to make sure that everyone fully understands each option.

If the group is able, invite them to generate the criteria that will be used to assess the options. If they lack the experience to do this, provide the criteria. For simplicity, it's best not to have more than 5 criteria. Note that the criteria will change depending on the subject being decided.

Explain the three-point system: high = 3 pts, medium = 2 pts, low = 1 pt. Allow quiet time while everyone thinks about how they want to rate each option against the criteria. When they've decided, invite students to go to the flip chart to post their scores.

When everyone has added their rating, add the scores and announce the results. Facilitate a conversation about how the use of criteria influenced their thinking on the final decision. Ratify the results.

The great thing about all of these *Multi-voting* techniques is that they are simple to use and create participation. They also help learners think analytically, which teaches them a multitude of ways to make important life decisions.

*Chapter Four: Decision-Making in the Classroom*

Traditional approaches to teaching rarely made use of decision-making tools. This was a missed opportunity, since students feel much more involved when they're consulted and are given a say.

**Online Decision Making**

With so many courses moving to the online space, it's important to understand that decision methods can be adapted to work with remote groups. In the following examples it's assumed that the students are all in separate locations and that you will not interact with them except though posted messages.

- Send an email that clarifies the topic/item to be decided upon and the decision method being used.
- Refer back to the various decision-making steps described earlier in this chapter. Create a questionnaire or page that allow people to type in their comments. Set a clear time frame for the idea-input phase.
- Once all ideas have been posted, ask students to review all comments.
- Ask students to download a decision-making app such as *Poll Everywhere, Slido* or *Kahoot.*
- Upload a summary of student comments.
- Invite students to vote based on the criteria selected.
- Encourage the kind of candid feedback that is enabled by the use of such platforms as *Google Forms, Mentimeter, Plicers*, etc.
- Send the tabulated results to the group.
- Set up a space on the share site so that students can comment on the results if further discussion is warranted.

*Facilitating in the Classroom*

# Chapter Five: Facilitating Through Conflict

Over the years, professional group facilitators have developed specific ways to manage group conflict. Chapter five will:

- describe how facilitators manage conflict
- demonstrate how to use *Norms* to set a positive climate
- explain how to make behavioral interventions
- identify a model for both giving and receiving feedback

## How Facilitators Manage Conflict

Unlike facilitators, teachers have much more authority to manage conflict. A teacher can order a student to stop a disruptive behavior, impose a detention, or send a student to the vice-principal's office. Since group facilitators have no authority over the people they're helping, they've developed non-confrontational approaches.

Before we delve into some of the specific conflict tools facilitators have developed, let's take a quick look at the general principles that they follow.

1. **Stay calm**: Maintain your composure, and don't raise your voice. Speak slowly and in an even tone. Avoid using emotional language.

2. **Watch your language**: Don't use loaded words like arguing, conflict, or even anger. This makes things sound worse than they are.

3. **Stay neutral**: Don't take sides or allow your body language to hint that you favor one person's perspective over another.

4. **Let people vent**: Invite students to calmly and slowly state their perspective on the dispute. Insist that they speak one at a time.

5. **Encourage calm:** If voices become raised, or people shout, stop the action and ask them to lower their voices and choose different words to get their message across.

6. **Emphasize listening**: Ask those in the dispute to paraphrase what the other party is saying. Don't move forward until each side indicates that their ideas have been understood.

7. **Seek solutions:** Ask each student to suggest ideas that could resolve the issue. If solutions aren't possible or relevant, ask them to at least acknowledge the valid points being made by the other party.

8. **End on a positive note:** Point out what has been gained from hearing each other out and/or finding solutions without anger.

## An Important Tip: Never, Ever Utter the Word Conflict!

Even though it's appropriate to use the word conflict in written materials, it's a bad idea to label any dispute using that word. Why? ….because that word has bad connotations. When you hear about conflict on the nightly news it's often in connection with destruction and people dying.

Describing a minor dispute as a conflict will elevate its seriousness. Instead choose words that downplay contention.

| **Instead of saying…** | **Say things like…** |
|---|---|
| *"Looks like you two are having a conflict."* | *"Looks like you have different ideas about this."* |
| | *"Different opinions are okay, as long as we hear both sides."* |

## Group *Norms*

In the same way that an ounce of prevention is worth a pound of cure, it's always best to create an environment where conflict is unlikely to occur in the first place. One way to do this is to engage students in setting rules that define how people ought to interact.

The behavioral science term for this is setting *Norms*. *Norms* are rules or guidelines that describe how people ought to behave and how things should ideally be done. When *Norms* are created before conflict they act as a preventative. When *Norms* are reset after a conflict, they help to ensure it doesn't happen again.

Don't confuse *Norms* with the rules and regulations created and imposed by a school or school board. These rules are often a safety necessity. *Norms* are something different. They're rules that describe how students want to interact inside their classrooms and project teams. With notable exceptions, *Norms* should always be created by the group members and are never dictated from outside.

*Facilitating in the Classroom*

The power of *Norms* lies in the fact that they come directly from the students. Having students set rules empowers them to create the environment they need to thrive. Engaging them in setting those rules also increases their buy-in to keeping those commitments.

*Norming* is extremely simple, but don't let its simplicity fool you. A set of rules that everyone has agreed to honor is a powerful way to prevent strife. Below are some examples of *Norming* questions for different situations.

## Classroom *Norms*

There are several ways to approach *Norm* development. If the group is mature, divide the class into groups of three. Ask them to discuss a set of specific *Norming* questions like the ones below. It's okay to provide a few as sample *Norms* so that students understand what you're looking for, but avoid the temptation to post and then impose rules without any participation. Remember that this is a decision-making conversation, so you'll need to make sure you hear from everyone and that everyone is asked if they can live with the final set of rules.

Here are some sample *Norming* questions appropriate to young learners:

- *"How would you like to be greeted at the start of the day?"*
- *"Is it ever okay to yell at another person? What should we do instead?"*
- *"What's the right thing to say or do when you want to borrow something from somebody?"*
- *"What's the rule if you want to say something to the whole class?"*
- *"How would you like to have people act while you're making a presentation?"*
- *"How should people behave while the teacher's speaking?"*
- *"Since side-chatting is distracting, what's the rule about that?"*
- *"What should the rule be about using cell phones during the class?"*
- *"Who's responsible for cleaning up at the end of the day?"*

If you don't think that the first approach will work, an alternate strategy is to post a set of potential *Norms.* Divide the class into discussion groups of three. Give a specific time frame for groups to identify which rules they think should be adopted.

Examples of classroom *Norms* to offer for consideration:

- Be enthusiastic.
- Be considerate.
- Be supportive of each other.
- Show respect.
- Have patience.
- Be open to the ideas of others.
- Listen attentively when others are speaking.
- Be welcoming so that everyone feels comfortable.

- Don't interrupt while someone else is speaking.
- Comment on another person's idea before countering them.
- Let others finish without interrupting.
- Don't hog the floor.
- Be considerate of feelings.
- Respect each other's space.
- Share helpful ideas.
- Never shout or yell.
- Include and help others.
- Offer notes and collect handouts for people who miss a class.
- Don't side-chat while someone is speaking.
- No cliques: include everybody.
- Don't pick on or make fun of anyone.

To end this activity, hand out voting dots or markers, and invite students to place their dots or check marks next to the rules they feel are most important. If there are twenty potential rules, give each person ten votes. Ask students not to vote more than once for a single item.

Tally the scores. After the class, rewrite the rules, placing the highest rated items at the top of the list. Drop any that received few or no votes. Post the *Norms* in the classroom and reference it at the start of group activities.

## Project Team *Norms*

Active learning often involves the creation of project teams. If these teams are meant to stay together for extended periods, they will need rules to stay on course and maintain positive relationships. These rules can be about how to manage work, how to treat each other, and how to deal with issues.

If the project team is mature, facilitate a conversation based on questions like the ones listed below. Remember that this is a decision-making conversation, so you'll need to check that every team member can live with all of the rules.

- *"What kind of atmosphere do we want on our team?"*
- *"How do we need to treat each other/talk to each other?"*
- *"What's the rule about meeting attendance?"*
- *"What do we do if someone misses a meeting or deadline?"*
- *"How do we ensure that workloads are fair and equal?"*
- *"How do we stay in touch during the project?"*
- *"How do we make changes to project parameters?"*
- *"What should we do if we find that we're starting to argue?"*
- *"What should we do if the team starts to miss important deadlines?"*

An alternative approach is to give new project teams a set of potential rules to consider. Distribute examples like those listed below. Allow time for the whole team to discuss the

*Facilitating in the Classroom*

rules and select the ones they feel are most important. Facilitate a discussion to ratify these rules, then make sure that every team member has a copy of the team *Norms*. Here are some rules to offer for consideration:

- Stay upbeat and enthusiastic about the project until the end.
- Attend all project meetings or study sessions.
- If you can't come to a meeting, notify others.
- Share workloads equally.
- Always be on time.
- Come to meetings prepared with completed assignments.
- Stay in touch with each other during the project.
- Help anyone who falls behind: be supportive.
- Make sure feedback is always constructive and not mean.
- Be flexible and agreeable to change.
- Be willing to revise dates, deadlines, and deliverables if necessary.

If a project team is very mature, they may be able to have this discussion without you present. Likewise, an online project team can do this exercise remotely, or via online chat. The key is to ensure that they send you their completed set of *Norms* and that they keep their rules in clear sight while working on their project.

## Safety Norms

If you're going to facilitate a hot topic, you'll need a special set of what are known as *Safety Norms.* These are rules designed to both create and maintain a calm and civil environment.

One way to start this conversation is to help learners understand the difference between a healthy debate and a dysfunctional argument. Point out that the ability to engage in a healthy debate is an essential life skill. Taking part in dysfunctional arguments, on the other hand, can lead to escalating hostility.

Begin by sharing the chart below. Then start a discussion with a focus on the dysfunctional behaviors. Ask students to talk about what happens when you do each of the things in the right-hand column. Then ask them to describe what happens when people follow the practices in the left-hand column instead.

| In Healthy Debates | In Dysfunctional Arguments |
|---|---|
| People are open to hearing others' ideas | People assume they're right. |
| People listen and respond to ideas, even if they don't agree with them. | People don't really listen, especially If they don't agree. |
| Everyone tries to understand the views of the other person. | No one is interested in how the other person sees the situation. |
| People stay objective and focus on the facts. | People get personally attacked and blamed. |
| There's a systematic approach to analyzing the situation and looking for solutions. | Hot topics just get thrashed around. |

Unlike with classroom *Norms,* where it's important to get the students to generate a set of rules, this is that rare situation when you should impose rules. Why? Because the rules of good conduct are non-negotiable during debates. Professional facilitators never allow groups to debate without a set of clear rules.

Below is a starter set of *Safety Norms.* Over time you may discover that additional rules are needed. To get buy-in to *Safety Norms,* form dyads to discuss why each rule is important. An alternate approach is to facilitate a large group discussion addressing why each rule is important.

*Facilitating in the Classroom*

> **"Why is it important to…**
>
> …stay objective and focus on the facts?
> …watch your tone of voice and body language?
> …listen actively to other people's ideas?
> …ensure you understand a point before you disagree?
> …debate ideas instead of attacking anyone personally?
> …offer a constructive suggestion Instead of criticizing?
> …never shout or get emotional?
> …never interrupt while someone else is speaking?
> …never engage in name calling or insults?
> …never make fun of other people or use sarcasm?
> …always admit when others are right?
> …congratulate opponents when they make a valid point?
> …accept good ideas coming from opponents?
> …end on a gracious note?"

Once everyone has acknowledged the rules, post them in clear sight. Once the debate is underway, never hesitate to stop the action anytime a *Safety Norm* has been broken. If anyone exhibits behavior that isn't appropriate, intervene quickly using the intervention language described on the next page.

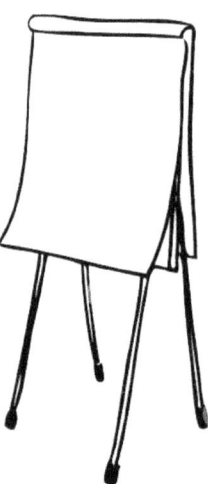

*Chapter Five: Facilitating Through Conflict*

# Behavioral Interventions

Facilitators never stand by and watch people argue or act out. Since they have no real power, they've developed a tactful way to intervene. Their approach is to use language very carefully to redirect poor behavior without making it personal. This approach works with all grade levels, but will be especially useful for college level instructors who teach mature students.

While most students behave themselves, there are times when ineffective behaviors occur. Some examples might include:

- side-chatting while a classmate is making a presentation
- fooling around during a group exercise
- looking at text messages during a group discussion
- using hostile language during a debate
- using sarcasm or making a personal attack
- yelling or using an angry tone of voice

A teacher can, of course, simply say: "*Jane, please put away that phone.*" or "*Alice, stop fidgeting.*" or "*I need all eyes on me right now.*"

There's nothing wrong with this kind of direct wording, especially when dealing with young children. It gets right to the point and describes the specific behavior that's appropriate. If students are more mature, however, it's more effective to redirect bad behaviors using the steps described below.

The key to this technique is to understand that no judgment is placed on the person who's acting out. Facilitators separate the person from the behavior. Instead of characterizing the person as bad, they simply focus on the fact that the way they're behaving isn't working.

Facilitators do this in three steps. First, they make the individual aware of what they're doing and then help them see that their current behavior is working against them. Finally they offer specific alternate actions.

---

1. **Describe what you see the other person doing to raise their awareness:**
   "*I see that you're….*" or "*I'm noticing that you're….*" or "*You're…..*"

2. **Describe the impact of the behavior as a concern for the other person:**
   "*I'm concerned that…*" or "*I'm worried that…*"

3. **Offer specific instructions about what you need them to do instead.**
   (Tell) "*I need you to….*" or (Ask) "*What should we do?…..*"

*Facilitating in the Classroom*

Let's take a closer look at what each of these statements accomplishes:

**Statement 1** raises awareness
**Statement 2** signals that you're acting out of concern for that person
**Statement 3** describes the specific behavior that would be better

Note that there are two options in step #3: You can tell or you can ask. If you think you're going to get a responsible suggestion from the student, you can <u>ask</u> for their solution. If you suspect that they aren't going to make a responsible suggestion about how they ought to behave, then you'll have to resort to <u>telling</u>.

It's important to note, that while it's best to use all three steps, it's okay to intervene using only statements 1 & 3, or only statements 2 & 3 or even just statement 3 all by itself. The key is not to drop step 3 since that's the all-important redirect.

Note that step 2 is deliberately supportive. If you take a look at the examples that follow, you will see how step 2 communicates concern.

## Behavioral Intervention Examples

As you will see from the following examples, intervening is respectful, specific and constructive. It's assertive without ever sounding aggressive.

Joe is really enthusiastic and always has a lot to say. The problem is that he barely listens to what anyone else has to say.

1. *"Joe, you've shared a lot of ideas."*
2. *"I'm worried that you're missing out on hearing what others think."*
3. *"Please hold off until you get to hear from others."*

Mary and Fred are locked in a circular argument. Each of them is repeating the same points over and over. Both are getting upset. You're concerned that they're not hearing each other.

1. *"Fred, Mary. I'm noticing that you're each repeating your points."*
2. *"I'm concerned that you may not be hearing each other's ideas."*
3. *"Let's start over. Fred, you go first, then Mary, you tell us what Fred's saying."*

The current small group report-back session is running long. You worry that there won't be time to hear from each group.

1. *" I need to point out that the report back session is running long."*
2. *"I'm concerned that you're not going to get out of here on time."*
3. *"Please present your team's top three findings only."*

*Chapter Five: Facilitating Through Conflict*

Jane just starts talking while another student is in the middle of an important point.

1. *"Excuse me Jane, but you started talking before Michael was finished."*
2. *"We don't want to miss out on anything either of you has to say."*
3. *"Please hold off until Michael has finished making his point."*

Brian is using a condescending tone of voice. Other students are getting upset.

2. *"Brian, I'm concerned that your tone of voice is getting in the way of people really hearing your ideas."*
3. *"Please restate that last point, using a slightly different tone."*

Two students are side-chatting loudly while another student is making a presentation.

1. *"Alex. Joe. I see you're in a conversation."*
2. *"I'm concerned that we're not getting your thoughts on this topic."*
3. *"We need you back."*

The group is in the middle of an important discussion when you notice that time is almost up. Everyone is behaving appropriately so you ask instead of tell.

1. *"I notice out that we're almost out of time for this topic."*
2. *"I would hate to end something that everyone thinks is really important."*
3. *"Should we wrap this up or should we adjust the agenda so that we can stay on this topic? Let's see a show of hands."*

Mateo is personally attacking Leo. Leo is becoming very upset.

1. *"Mateo. You are making comments about Leo."*
3. *"Please start over and this time tell Leo how you disagree with his idea instead of saying anything about him personally."*

## *Norm*-based Interventions

The great thing about having a set of *Norms* is that you can use them to restore effective behaviors. Here are a few examples of how that sounds:

Whenever Alan hears something that he doesn't like, he raises his voice. This is very intimidating and creates a lot of tension.

1. *"Alan, you're shouting."*
2. *"That breaks one of the classroom rules."*
3. *"Please lower your voice."*

*Facilitating in the Classroom*

For the third time today, Anne is looking at text messages during an important demonstration.

1. " Anne, I notice that you're texting."
2. "This class created a rule about that."
3. "Please wait until recess to look at your messages."

Jake is about to leave without helping clean up after the craft session.

1. "Looks like you are getting ready to leave, Jake."
2. "Remember that the class agreed that everyone needs to help clean up."
3. "Please get the broom and sweep the floors."

## Body Language Interventions

Often people don't verbalize how they're feeling, but their body language speaks volumes. When facilitators see concerned looks, anger, or yawns, they use an abbreviated version of the three-step intervention model to surface unspoken feelings.

This formula has two steps. In step one, you state what you see without making any judgments. In step two, options are offered. These options send the signal that it's okay to pick one. It also sends the message that you're looking for solutions and not being confrontational.

**Body Language Interventions**

1. Describe what you see…

    *"I see that you're frowning."*

2. Ask what it means and offer alternatives…

    *"Tell me what that means: Did we miss something? Did we get something wrong?"*

## Body Language Intervention Examples

Adam looks really upset and isn't saying anything. He has totally withdrawn.

1. "Adam, you look concerned?"
2. "Has someone made a point you don't agree with? Is there an important idea that we missed?"

Marianne keeps shuffling through her papers. She's completely distracted.

1. "Marianne, you're shuffling through your papers."
2. "Are you missing a page? Have you lost your place? Can I help?"

Miguel looks puzzled.

1. "Miguel, I see a puzzled look. Tell us what that means."
2. "Is there something you find confusing? Do you have a question that needs to be answered?"

The class has been going on for some time, with lots of small group presentation. The whole group looks tired and people are yawning. Energy levels have dropped.

1. " I see some yawns and a couple of you are sagging in your seats."
2. "Tell me what that means and what should we do about it? Should we try to speed things up or should we stop for a break?"

Folks who aren't familiar with facilitation, sometimes labor under the mistaken impression that facilitators are unassertive because they stay neutral about the subject being discussed. While facilitators are definitely unassertive about <u>what</u> is being discussed, they are never neutral about <u>how</u> the discussion is unfolding.

Whenever proceedings become ineffective, they don't hesitate to point it out and offer alternative approaches. If a group isn't working within time limits, they ask how that problem can be fixed. If people behave inappropriately, they assertively redirect their behavior. Facilitation is not a passive activity!

> Facilitators are unassertive about the content
> but are very assertive about the process.

*Facilitating in the Classroom*

## Giving and Receiving Feedback

Feedback is the process of providing information about past performance with the positive goal of helping individuals improve. It's especially important to teach feedback skills to student, who will be working in teams so that they can use those skills when issues arise.

Feedback is always meant to be constructive: It is never done to criticize or offend. Regardless of the situation, follow these guidelines:

- **Check the facts** - Ensure your understanding is accurate and fair. Investigate actual events to avoid misjudging the situation.
- **Time it -** Offer the feedback as soon as possible after the situation to be discussed.
- **Find a private space** - Hold the feedback session somewhere that's both private and free from distractions.
- **Be personally present** - Sit or stand close to the person. Make eye contact and be attentive to what the other person says.
- **Be specific instead of general** - Describe exactly what happened, so that facts, not impressions, form the basis of the feedback.
- **Be descriptive rather than evaluative** - Tell the other person what you've noticed or what's happened. Avoid any judgmental comments or personal labels.
- **Let the other person explain** - Gain their perspective on the matter.
- **Demonstrate caring** - Use language that conveys your positive intention to be helpful and supportive.
- **Focus on what can be changed** - Suggest improvements that the other person is capable of implementing.
- **End on a positive note** - Reaffirm your desire to maintain a positive relationship.

If a pair of students approaches you to complain about each other, teach the students the steps of the feedback process. Then bring them together to share feedback while you remain in the neutral facilitator role. To ensure that the feedback session is effective, give the students the guidelines on the following page. It includes wording examples to help students understand the kind of language that they need to use. Remember to set *Safety Norms* before you stage this conversation to ensure a positive climate (page 73).

# Feedback Guidelines

### Step 1: Ask Permission to Offer Feedback.
State your interest in sharing feedback. .

> *"I'd like to tell you about something that happened yesterday that I think we need to discuss and try to resolve."*

### Step 2: Specifically Describe What Happened.
Give a clear and specific description of what has happened. Use objective-sounding language. Avoid generalizing, exaggerating or offering emotional accounts.

> *"At yesterday's meeting, you didn't have your part of the presentation ready to share with the rest of us. This is the third time that you've come to a project meeting without your assignment complete."*

### Step 3: Explain the Direct Impact of the Individual's Actions.
Describe the impact on individuals, the program, or the department. Keep it very objective and don't get personal. Avoid blaming. Deal with the facts of the current situation.

> *"I'm worried that we're going to miss our project deadline. Being late will lower everyone's grades."*

### Step 4: Offer the Opportunity to Explain.
Invite the person receiving the feedback to share their perspective. Listen actively; use attentive body language and paraphrase key points even when you don't agree, to demonstrate that you're listening.

> *"Please tell me what happened from your perspective."*

### Step 5: Draw Ideas out of the Other Person.
Frame the dialogue as an opportunity to make improvements. Give the other person the opportunity to propose solutions before you offer your ideas. This will allow you to gauge how much self-awareness they have about the situation.

> *"What do you suggest so that this doesn't continue?"*

### Step 6: Offer Specific Suggestions for Improvement.
Make suggestions that will improve the situation. Wherever possible, build on the ideas that the other person has already put forward.

> *"I like your idea to create a writing schedule. How about one of us touching base with you a few days before each deadline to see if you need help or are running into any blocks."*

**Step 7: Summarize and Express Your Support.**
Demoralizing people never helps, so it's important to offer encouragement and end on an optimistic note.

> "Thank you for being willing to talk about this. I'm glad that we have a plan!"

**Step 8: Follow Up**
Feedback is only effective if it actually leads to change. Be sure to end the feedback session with clear action steps. This eliminates the necessity to repeat the whole exercise.

> "I'll call you the week before our next meeting to see if you're on track to have everything done, or if you need help from the team."

## Receiving Feedback with Grace

Feedback is about give and take; sometimes we're on the receiving end. A core facilitator practice is to invite specific feedback at the end of every engagement.

Since most people find it difficult to offer feedback, it's important to make this easier for others. Here are some guidelines for what to do when you're on the receiving end of feedback:

- **Be open and accepting** - Even if you don't like the idea of getting feedback, act like you're fine with it.

    > "I'm always ready to find out how I can improve."

- **Try to avoid becoming emotional** - Breathe deeply. Sit back. Adopt a relaxed body posture. Lower your voice. Speak slowly.

    > "Tell me what you think I'm not doing right."

- **Listen actively** - Make eye contact with the speaker. Paraphrase what they're saying even if you don't agree.

    > "So, you're saying that I'm just doing my own thing and not following the project plan that we created at our first meeting."

- **Ask Questions** - Ask follow-on questions to get more details about their perspective on the situation.
-
    > "Can you describe some recent examples?"

- **Don't get defensive** - Understand the other person's perspective before presenting your side of the story. Ask for more details.

*Chapter Five: Facilitating Through Conflict*

*"I understand what you're saying about me being independent. What can I do to fix this?"*

- **Offer solutions** – Acknowledge the other person's solutions, then offer up suggestions of your own. Make sure to respond to what the other student wants, or they'll feel that you're ignoring their needs.

    *"Maybe at the end of our project meetings, I should be the one who summarizes the decisions that were made."*

- **Thank the student who provided the feedback** - Unless the feedback session was cruel or conducted with negative intention, thank the person who took the time to offer feedback.

    *"I really appreciate that you took the time to tell me about this and help me fix it."*

- **Work to improve** - If you acknowledge feedback and then ignore it, the relationship with the other person will worsen.

    *"You're going to see that I'm more of a team player."*

- **Follow up** - Periodically let those who have given you feedback know what you're doing in response to their input.

    *"Am I doing better at staying on our team plan?"*

Managing differences is a lot easier with the right tools. Clear *Norms* and assertive intervention strategies are invaluable in maintaining a positive culture in the classroom.

*Facilitating in the Classroom*

# Chapter Six: Building Strong Teams

A good deal of active learning takes place in teams. While some teams are only together for a short time, others last for weeks and even months. To support your work with teams, this chapter will:

- explain why teams need structure in order to be effective
- examine the stages of team development
- describe the specific discussions needed to properly launch a team
- identify strategies for intervening if team members become embroiled in conflict

## Teams Need Structure

One of the biggest mistakes to make when launching a new project team is to assume that the members will automatically know how to function as a cohesive unit. In fact, most teams don't run smoothly for very long. Studies of team life cycles show that teams go through the following predictable stages:

1) *Forming:* This is the optimistic, honeymoon stage when energy is high and people are still on their best behavior.
2) *Storming:* This is when the going gets tough, when people start to irritate each other and/or when team members fail to do their share of the work
3) *Norming:* This is a re-grouping phase. Team members are brought together to identify issues and develop strategies to get back on track. This discussion often includes personal feedback so that team members can adjust their behavior.
4) *Performing:* This is a stage of high performance that teams achieve when their issues have been resolved and everything is running smoothly.
5) *Adjourning:* This is a discussion or celebration to bring closure to the team once the project is complete.

Teams can go directly from the *Forming* to the *Performing* stage, but it's rare.
In fact, *Storming* is so common that it's practically guaranteed to take place. This is especially true if the team doesn't have a strong foundation. This foundation is commonly called a *Team Charter*. Charters are created during discussions in which team members establish rules, clarify roles, and set work parameters.

If a team lasts long enough, *Storming* can occur more than once. Teams get derailed for different reasons at different times. Regardless of the cause, it's important to understand that *Storming* rarely fixes itself. Most teams that experience periods of strife need guidance to get back on track. Without the right intervention, *Storming* is usually the demise of a team.

*Chapter Six: Building Strong Teams*

Teams that are together for only a few hours don't need a *Team Charter*. Having a solid set of *Norms* like those on page 71 and clarity about roles, deliverables and timeframes should do the trick. Teams working on complex activities or for longer periods will, however, need to be properly launched.

In workplaces that use teams a lot, a structured team formation discussion is always conducted. This conversation helps ensure that the team gets off to a strong start and doesn't fall apart the first time it hits a bump in the road.

Below are the elements of the comprehensive team launch discussion to create a *Team Charter*. This set of conversations can be facilitated in a few hours for a team with three to five members. Of course, it can take longer for bigger teams.

This conversation is ideally conducted face-to-face. If team members are working in remote locations, however, post the guidelines on the team share-site. Allow time for review, then facilitate an online discussion of the *Charter* topics.

---

***Team Charter* Components**

1. Personal and skills profile
2. Team goal
3. Team rules
4. Decision making
5. Roles and responsibilities
6. Communication plan

---

1. **Personal and skills profile:** This conversation helps students get comfortable and discover each other's strengths. A fun way to start is to invite people to share a favorite picture, and then describe what that picture says about them.

    - Invite each student to introduce themselves. This can include anything they choose to share about their family life, hobbies, sports, favorite vacation, most fun thing to do with friends, etc. Ask each student to identify the skills that they bring to the team. This can be anything from report writing to organizing skills.

2. **Team Goal:** The basic glue that holds all teams together is everyone striving to achieve the same goal. It's common to assume that everyone automatically knows what the team is trying to achieve, but this isn't always the case. In fact, team member often have slightly different impressions about the project goal. To ensure that everybody is on the same page, do the following:

- Hand out a clear and detailed team goal statement. This needs to include what the team is expected to accomplish and by when. Specify the deliverables such as a final report, exhibit or presentation. Outline the dates for all deliverables or activities.

- Facilitate a discussion about each element. *Is everyone clear about exactly what's expected and involved? Are there any suggestions, comments or amendments? Is anything missing?*

- Invite each student to state what they hope to personally gain from helping the team achieve its goal. This includes the skills, experiences and friendships that they hope to gain.

A good way to end the discussion about the group goal is to create a team name. If the team's going to be entering a competition at the end of their project, they might want to also create a logo or coat of arms. These visuals help give the team an identity.

3. **Roles and Responsibilities:** Confusion about who's doing what is a sure formula for disaster. To avoid this, break the project down into its key components. If the group is young, prepare a chart of tasks in advance of the meeting. More mature students can be facilitated through a discussion to identify project elements. Once you have a chart:

    - Facilitate a discussion to identify the sub-tasks and skills needed for each task. You could also create a scale that rates each task:
    (1 = easy, 2 = moderate, 3 = difficult).

    - Ask the team to suggest who should take the lead for which project elements. The difficulty scale will help you ensure that no one ends up with all the difficult or complex tasks.

    - Identify clear timelines for each task or phase of the project.

    - End by checking that everyone can live with the role distribution.

4. **Team Rules:** Teams often collapse from infighting. The best thing that you can do to prevent this is to make sure that the team has a clear set of *Norms*. Utilize the process outlined on page 71. In addition to what's on those pages, here are a few additional tips.

    - If the team is composed of more mature students use the *Norming* questions shown on page 71. If team members are younger, provide the sample rules on page 70. In either case, facilitate a discussion about why each of the rules is important. Always leave the door open so that students can suggest additional rules.

*Chapter Six: Building Strong Teams*

- Record the team's *Norms* on a piece of flip chart paper. Ask someone to take custody of this page. That person should bring the *Norms* page to all team meetings. Everyone should take a photo of the *Norms* so that they're easy to access.

- Suggest that the team periodically start their meetings with this conversation: *"Are we breaking any of our rules? Do we need to add any new rules?"*

5. **Decision making:** Teams can be very confused about which decisions they can make and which they can't. They can also be confused about how to make decisions. The conversation about decision making is one that most teams need to have more than once during a lengthy project. Here are some things to clarify right at the start:

    - <u>Empowerment:</u> Hand out clear written guidelines that describe which decisions team members can make on their own, and which decisions need approval from a teacher.

    - <u>Decision methods:</u> Review the decision-methods described starting on page 53. Ask the group to have a discussion about which methods they should use to make which types of decisions.

6. **Communication Plan:** Team members need to be able to contact each other. In an era when most students have a cell phone this is easy. If you want them to call you rather than each other, this needs to be clarified.

    - If it's okay for team members to call each other, create a contact page that lists cell numbers. Clarify if they ought to call or text.

    - If students need to call you instead, specify when they can make those calls.

    - Ask students to identify any additional rules or limits about contacting each other.

Make notes about the agreements reached by the team. A more mature team can type up their own notes. When the *Team Charter* summary is complete, circulate it to everyone who needs to be in the loop.

*Facilitating in the Classroom*

## Team *Storming*

Unfortunately, even teams that have been properly launched, can nonetheless break down. Some of the most common causes and symptoms of *Storming* are:

- A few people are doing all the work, while others make excuses.
- Some members lack the skills needed to complete assigned tasks.
- The team lacks some of the resources it needs.
- A couple of team members have gone off to pursue the part of the project that they find interesting. They no longer work on the rest of the project.
- There's a lot of arguing about how to proceed.
- Decision-making conversations go in circles.
- Some team members have started disliking each other.
- Cohesion is gone and cliques have formed.
- Some people no longer speak to other members of the team.
- Deadlines are being missed and people blame each other.

When these sorts of dysfunctions happen, it's important to intervene. Why? Because these things simply will not fix themselves. Since intervening is a delicate task, it's important to take a structured approach. Just giving team members a pep talk, or stepping in to take control, is not going to resolve complex issues. To really fix things, you have to involve team members in discussions that get the team back on track. Below is a description of how professional facilitators help teams through *Storming*.

They begin by gathering data about what's actually going on. Facilitators talk to team members one-on-one. They never act on the perspective of just one person. The other thing they often do is to sit in on a team meeting to observe the group dynamics. Are a few people doing all the talking? Are they following their team rules? Are they getting bogged down whenever they try to make decisions?

After they've drilled down to root causes, facilitators look at the team's issues through the prism of the following intervention model.

## The Team Intervention Model

This model sorts team issues into six categories. Each type of issue has an accompanying set of intervention strategies. The easiest things to fix are at the top of the model. The more difficult items are at the bottom.

Team building experts always tackle what's at the top of the model first because fixing the easy stuff often straightens out the sensitive interpersonal issues.

**Team Problem Category 1**. The team parameters, such as the goal, deliverables, and timeframes, have become unclear or are no longer relevant. A few people are ignoring the tasks originally assigned to them and are doing their own thing.

**Intervention:** Bring the team together to take a look at the parameters the team ratified in their *Team Charter*. Facilitate a discussion to update any tasks, dates, or deliverable that have gone out of focus. Note that this is a decision-making conversation, so check in with everyone at every step. The revised parameters need to be a consensus to ensure total buy-in.

**Team Problem Category 2.** Some team members lack specific skills. These can be task-related skills, or they can be interpersonal skills. The team might also be unable to make group decisions or know how to have a debate without arguing.

**Intervention:** Identify the specific skills that are lacking. Arrange for training, coaching, or mentoring to upgrade the missing skills. If the team lacks group skills, you may need to sit in on a few team meetings to share the difference between arguments and debates (page 68), or hold a brief session about how to make group decisions (page 55).

**Team Problem Category 3.** Some people on the team are behaving in ways that are upsetting others. The team *Norms* are either being ignored or are inadequate to manage the challenges being encountered.

**Intervention:** At a team meeting, post the original set of team rules. Number the *Norms*. Hand each person a strip of voting dots. Ask each person to separately mark each dot with the number of any *Norm* that is not being followed. Collect all the dots. Ask for a volunteer to post the dots. This will show you which rules are being broken.

Post a blank sheet of flip chart paper. Facilitate a discussion based on questions like: *"Which rules is the team successfully following?"* Record those rules. Look at the results of the voting exercise about which rules are not being followed. Ask: *"Are these still important? Why? Why are they not being followed? Which rules need to be updated? Does the wording need to be changed? Are there new situations that you didn't anticipate at the start of the project? Describe any new rules that need to be added."*

End by reviewing the revised *Norms*. Ask team members to describe the specific actions and behaviors that would be going on if each rule were being followed. For each *Norm* on the updated list ask: *"What does it look like if this rule is being followed?"*

Remember that this is a decision-making conversation, so check in with everyone to validate the new *Norms*. This has to be a consensus to ensure total buy-in.

**Team Problem Category 4.** Progress is being blocked by a problem or barrier. This type of issue has nothing to do with the team parameters, member skills, or group behavior. Some examples of this type of problem: the team isn't able to book enough time in the computer lab, team members don't all have the same software, so they can't share files, one of the team members lives really far away and can't stay for after school meetings.

*Facilitating in the Classroom*

**Intervention:** Facilitate a problem-solving discussion. Use the steps of the *Systematic Problem Solving Model* on page 126. This basically involves naming the problem that is blocking the team. Then, invite team members to describe every aspect of the current situation. This is followed by getting team members to brainstorm solutions. Once you have a list of potential solutions, use *Multi-voting* to help team members identify which solutions they think ought to be implemented. Finally, help them to identify who will do what, by when. Remember that you can make suggestions during the *Brainstorming* stage without losing your neutrality, as long as team members ratify your suggestions. End by identifying the action steps needed to resolve what's blocking team progress.

**Team Problem Category 5.** There's a dispute or bad feelings between two or more members of the team. People are arguing or are avoiding interaction.

**Intervention:** Sometimes even if you clarify the parameters, provide training, revamp the *Norms,* and solve problems, you still end up with people who can't get along. When this happens, you may need to conduct a *Needs and Offers Dialogue.*

This is a private conversation in which each team member is given a turn to tell the other party what they need from them in order to work together effectively again. No one is allowed to tell their side of the story. Looking back and rehashing what happened is a huge mistake that only serves to refresh the dispute. Instead, each person gets to state what they need from the other person <u>in the future</u> in order to be able to work together.

Bring the students who are in the dispute into a private space. Flip a coin to determine who speaks first. While one person is speaking the other person can't interrupt, argue back, or use dismissive body language. Listeners must make eye contact and take notes. Each party is only allowed to express*: "What I need from you going forward in order to productively work with each other is…"*

After both parties have taken a turn stating their needs, allow for a few minutes of quiet time so that students can write out offers. These are the things that they're willing to do in response to the needs expressed by the other person.

Invite team members to take turns exchanging offers. If these are accepted then bring closure. If someone says that an offer is insufficient to resolve the rift, ask the other party to offer more. Do this until both parties are satisfied. Even though you're neutral throughout, it's okay for you to suggest more appropriate language or ask that weak offers are strengthened so that they are effective at ending the dispute.

Once both parties signal that they've received acceptable offers, record these on a flip chart or whiteboard. Take a photo of these notes and circulate them to both parties. Before adjourning, set a date for the two parties to meet to check in on progress. Kn

**Team Problem Category 6.** An individual on the team is underperforming, acting out, or unable to complete their work. None of the previous five types of intervention activities have resolved the situation.

**Intervention:** Determine the underlying reason for the conduct. Bring that person in for a private session of structured feedback. Use the process described on page 81 for this one-on-one meeting. If the problem is too serious to be resolved by structured feedback, you may need to remove this student from the team, or refer them for counseling.

## The *Performing* Stage

Once *Storming* has been resolved, teams enter what is known as the *Performing* stage. This phase is characterized by the following traits:

- Everybody is clear about the goal of the team, the deadlines and the deliverables.
- Workloads are evenly distributed and everyone is contributing.
- There's a clear set of group *Norms* that are being followed.
- The team knows how to make decisions: which decisions they're empowered to make on their own, and which one's need to be approved.
- The team members communicate effectively. Everybody's in the loop.
- Tasks are being accomplished on time. The team is on track with its deliverables.
- People get along. There's a lot of mutual support and a sense of team spirit.

The *Performing* stage is great, but don't get complacent. Even teams that are running smoothly can slide back into Storming. That's why it's important to always monitor team progress.

## *Adjourning* the Team

At the end of any lengthy project, it's important to bring the members together to achieve closure. This is a time to celebrate success and say goodbye.

You can of course just have a pizza party. If you want to do something more personal, here are a few suggestions:

- Give each person a piece of poster-board. Have them write their name on their board. Tape the boards around the room at the farewell party. During the party, invite people to roam around posting positive comments about what each person contributed. People can also post pictures that they took during the project. This activity can easily be done online for teams that have worked from remote locations.

- Give out homemade trophies and awards for fun categories like most willing to work through the night, the person who brought the most snacks, the person who made the least excuses, and so forth.

*Facilitating in the Classroom*

- For a more serious wrap-up, facilitate a structured project review. This is based on three straightforward questions:

    1) What did we do really well? What went smoothly?
    2) What didn't we do that well? What was challenging?
    3) What lessons did we learn that will help us do better next time?

This last conversation will do a great deal to encourage team members to reflect, accept feedback and become more effective members of future teams.

Effective teamwork is a critically important part of experiential learning. That's because so much student-led learning takes place in small groups. Working on team projects gives students the opportunity to take charge: to set goals, manage deadlines, conduct research and interpret findings. Teamwork also imparts critically important social skills. Students have to communicate and collaborate with each other. It affords opportunities to work harmoniously with those who have different values and ideas. That's why maintaining team effectiveness is a key role of every facilitative teacher.

# Chapter Seven: Learning Design

Experiential learning isn't just about leading discussions, it also requires a major focus on how learning activities are designed and how group members are organized. To help you create engaging learning activities, this chapter will:

- describe room arrangements that encourage group dialogue
- identify optional group configurations
- explore a variety of ways to use learning teams
- describe activities that make lectures more engaging
- share tips about managing timed activities
- identify options for sharing group learning

## Essential Supplies

Making greater use of participative technique may require a few supplies you haven't used in the past.

### Flip chart paper/whiteboards

Anytime you facilitate a group discussion, you will need to record student comments either on pads of flip chart paper or on a whiteboard. If the budget allows, it's worthwhile to acquire at least one flip chart stand. If not sheets can be taped to a whiteboard, SMARTBoards or to walls.

Since pads of flip chart paper can be expensive, consider installing additional whiteboards. Students can write on the boards, then use their smart phones to take photos of any notes they want to keep.

### Tape

If you use flip chart paper that isn't self-stick you will need rolls of blue or green painter's tape. This type of tape won't damage walls or leave a residue.

### Markers

Whenever anyone writes on a flip chart or whiteboard they will need to use a marker. Be sure to buy chisel-tip markers, not pointed tip. If you use whiteboards you will need to purchase dry-erase markers.

### Index Cards or Scrap Squares

There are a number of activities that utilize index cards to collect ideas. For the budget conscious, cut scrap paper into small rectangles or squares.

**Stick-on Voting Dots**

To conduct *Multi-voting* activities, you'll need to purchase sheets of adhesive dots at a stationary store. These dots were created to mark file folders in medical offices. The dots come on sheets. Before you use them, you'll need to cut the sheets into strips so that they're ready to be distributed. If adhesive dots aren't in the budget, use small sticky note pads or scraps of paper and tape.

**A *Parking Lot* Sheet**

Tape a blank sheet of flip chart paper to a side wall. Write the words *Parking Lot* at the top of this page. When learners ask questions that you would rather have them answer for themselves, write them on the *Parking Lot* sheet. At the end of each meeting, review the items in the *Parking Lot* to see if the learners have discovered the answer for themselves. Answer only the questions that have them stumped.

**A Smartphone or Tablet**

Eliminate the need to collect flip chart paper by taking photos of the notes to share by texting or by posting them to *Google Classroom* or another platform.

**Countdown Timer**

To control time during group activities, download a free countdown timer app. Display the timer during all small group activities. This is very important!

**Software**

One of the simplest ways to engage learners in decision making is to use voting or polling software. Some current examples include *Slido, Kahoot, Pic Stitch*, and *polleverywhere*. Of course, these apps change all the time, so you should always check for the latest. Once you've selected a voting app, inform students so that they can download it well in advance of the class. In addition some SMARTBoards have a polling function as part of their applications package.

**Wall Décor**

Another important adjustment is to stop posting so much students' work. Elementary and middle school teachers spend hours decorating their classrooms to demonstrate their support and appreciation. This is a positive thing to do, but can be overdone. This is especially true when wall space is so occupied with yesterday's work that it leaves no room for today's conversation.

Consider freeing wall space for active learning, rather than using it exclusively for static displays. These changes make the class space more organic, which mirrors the more messy and emergent nature of experiential learning.

*Chapter Seven: Learning Decisions*

## Physical Layout

Participative learning requires a change in classroom layout. Tables and chairs in experiential classrooms are not arranged in rows, but are moved around to enable students to work in a variety of small group configurations.

Elementary schools are leaders in creating flexible classrooms. In high schools, space is far less flexible. By college, classrooms are often stuck in the formal "sit and listen" mode with chairs bolted into concrete, all turned to the front. It's both ironic and sad that the more mature the students, the less experiential learning methods are used.

To create engagement, classrooms need small tables and light chairs that can easily be moved around by the students. Some of the most common configurations for experiential learning activities are:

> A large U-shaped table for when holding presentations. This promotes discussion among the participants since they can all see each other. Small tables can, of course, be arranged to form a large "U" shape.

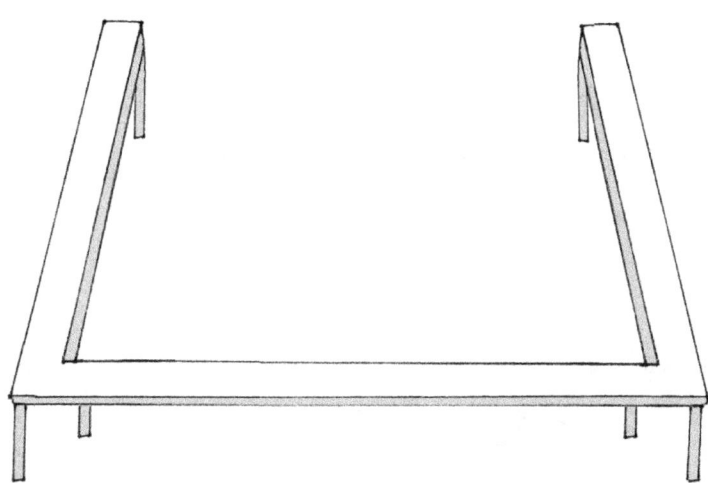

**U-Shaped Table**

*Facilitating in the Classroom*

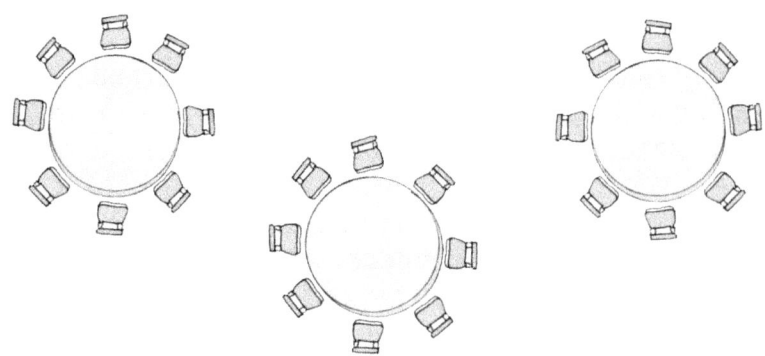

**Small Cluster of Tables and Chairs**

**Chairs Clustered Near Flip Charts**

**Chairs Clustered for Close Conversation**

*Chapter Seven: Learning Decisions*

## Ways to Organize Learners

One of the hallmarks of experiential learning is that people move around a lot. Besides the core seating layouts described on the previous page, here are a few more ways to arrange learners.

**Learning Partners** – The simplest and most efficient way to implement active learning is to divide the class into pairs or dyads. These learning partnerships can last for just one activity, or for a whole term. Below are a few of the things learning partners can do:

1. Discuss the findings of an assigned reading, exercise or video.
2. Practice a skill, such as coaching or giving feedback.
3. Recap a lecture or demonstration to create a joint summary.
4. Answer a question posed by the teacher.
5. Develop questions to ask the teacher.
6. Analyze a case scenario, or solve a problem.
7. Prepare for tests, or answer a quiz.
8. Compare how each person approached or completed a task.
9. Read and critique each other's written work.
10. Conduct an experiment.

**Speed Meetings** – This novel way to use partners is both active and very effective. Speed meetings are structured like speed dating. After learners have finished listening to a lecture, seeing a video, or working in small groups, invite each person to find a partner. People can sit or stand while they share their observations. Set a timer. After four or five minutes ask everyone to find a new partner. Keep moving people every four to five minutes. Repeat as desired.

In their short chats each person shares what they learned from the original activity and from other people in the speed chats.

When the speed meeting is over, the teacher facilitates a large group discussion to share key ideas in the large group. The teacher can then build on what students reported by adding additional information.

*Facilitating in the Classroom*

**Grouping and Re-grouping** – Form learners into small groups of from three to five participants. Allow four to six minutes for these groups to discuss the topic or specific questions that have been posed. When time is up, ask groups to call out the topic that became the main focus of their discussion. Invite people to leave these first groups if they think that they fit better somewhere else. Keep allowing students to regroup until everyone is in a group that's aligned with their interests.

**Two-four-eight** – Post a question. Ask each person to find a partner. Allow dyads from four to six minutes to discuss the question. Ask each dyad to link to another dyad. Allow from six to eight minutes for the foursomes to share their thoughts. Ask each foursome to join another foursome. Allow ten to twelve minutes for the groups of eight to share and also prioritize their ideas. Facilitate a discussion to share ideas.

**Wandering Flip Charts** – Write one question, math equation, or study topic per flip chart sheet. Post these around the room. Divide the class into even groups and ask them to cluster around different charts. Groups discuss and record their thoughts about the posted topic or equation. Use a timer that signals that it's time to move along. Groups circulate from chart to chart, reading what others have written and adding their thoughts to the mix. Keep groups moving until they've visited all of the flip charts. Hold a plenary to share highlights.

**Peer Coaching** – Students who excel in a particular subject are asked to help their fellow students. Consider a math class in which a handful of students are getting high grades, while others struggle. Place the proficient students at small tables. Assign a specific problem or equation to each table. Send a small group of students to each table. Allow twenty to thirty minutes while coaches share how they tackled the equation or problem. Learners who won't raise their hand to ask for help in front of the whole class will be much more likely to ask questions in a small group.

**Affinity Charting** – Create sub-categories that relate to the topic being studied. Form small discussion groups of from four to six students. Allow ten to fifteen minutes for students to discuss various aspects of the topic. Distribute blank index cards and markers. Ask group members to record their comments on the cards. Ask students to post these cards on the walls based on the sub-categories. When all of the cards are posted, move around the room and read the cards aloud. Invite students to elaborate. Give a lecture as you move around the room, all the while weaving in student ideas. For a diagram of an Affinity Diagram see page 120.

**Learning Teams** – A common way to organize an experiential learning activity is to create learning teams that focus on a specific situation or subject. Below is an example of how to use learning teams in a film class. This approach can, of course, be adapted to any subject that can be broken into sub-topics. Note that in this process, lectures still take place, however, they are offered <u>after</u> student exploration.

**Step 1** – Flip chart sheets are posted around the room. Each flip chart features a different topic. These could be headers, such as how characters are developed, how time is advanced, how the director transitions from one scene to the next, how music is used to support the plot, how suspense is created, how the director links various plot strands together to form a coherent ending, and so forth.

**Step 2** – Students divide themselves evenly among the flip charts. These small groups gather to chat about the specific aspect of filmmaking described on the chart in front of them. They identify the things that they're curious about or want to learn. They record their interests and questions. If the learners are young, the teacher can place a few starter questions on each flip chart sheet to get things going.

**Step 3** – After four or five minutes, everyone moves along to the next flip chart. Learners read the notes made by the previous group and add their thoughts and questions. Learners keep circulating until they've been to all of the charts.

**Step 4** - Ask students to remain standing when they get back to their original chart. Ask one person at each flip chart to read out the thoughts and questions related to each sub-topic. Invite students to take a photo of the notes on their chart.

**Step 5** - Provide a brief lecture about the key features of cinematography. Build on what students have already identified, adding elements that they missed.

**Step 6** - Learners watch the film, paying special attention to their focus area.

**Step 7** – Focused learning teams meet to discuss their observations. They summarize what they noticed and record their observations on flip chart paper.

**Step 8** - Each team makes a short presentation of their observations. The teacher facilitates a discussion that encourages students to connect the insights gained in the separate groups.

*Facilitating in the Classroom*

**Step 9** - The teacher gives a lecture about the filmmaking process to reinforce student discoveries, and provide information that the students missed.

An alternative way to share insights is to create discussion groups made up of one person from each focus team. These mixed groups combine their observations to create a complete picture of how the film functioned. This approach can eliminate the need for large group presentations.

Learning teams allows students to discover information that's traditionally shared through lectures. It can be used for any topic that can be broken down into sub-components. In a history class, learners can explore all of the factors that contributed to a significant historical event. Students in a social studies class can delve into the various factors that contribute to community health, and so forth.

**Study Prep Teams** – Studying for exams is a lonely activity. An alternate approach is to create prep teams in advance of an exam. The concept can be applied to exams in most subjects and can be done in person or online.

**Step 1** – Form teams of no more than four students. Create mock exam questions. Inform the teams that the mock questions are similar to those that will be on the actual test.

**Step 2** – Each member of the prep team takes responsibility for their share of the mock questions or topics. They commit to preparing written answers.

**Step 3** – Students are given time to research and prepare their responses. They may share rough notes or seek advice from each other during the research phase.

**Step 4** – Students meet to share their notes on the agreed to date. They bring copies of their summaries to distribute to teammates. At this meeting, they take turns walking each other through the material. They also discuss alternative answers.

**Step 5** – Each student takes the test on their own.

The use of study prep teams often results in a more thorough review of the material. It also avoids the pitfall of last-minute cram-sessions, since study teams need to get their work done well in advance of final tests. Students who tend to make excuses to teachers are far less likely to let their classmates down.

**Action Research Teams** – This format has learners doing research by conducting experiments or going on field trips. As the name suggests the data gathering is intended to end in tangible action steps. The example provided below is for a career guidance class whose aim is to investigate potential careers at a nearby company.

**Step 1** – The teacher contacts a large organization to request participation in the action research project. The teacher requests a list of staff job descriptions.

**Step 2** – Job titles and job descriptions are distributed to the students. Those interested in working in those jobs sign up for the field trip.

**Step 3** – Students decide which roles most interest them. Pairs of students attach themselves to each job. During class time, partners are given ten to fifteen minutes to identify the questions they would like to ask about that position. In the days before the site visit, students research their selected job on the Internet. They look up the educational requirements, responsibilities, time commitments, and salaries of their selected positions.

**Step 4** – Students go on a field trip to the company where they interview and shadow the staff for a day or for a special event. They spend time with the people doing the jobs that interest them to learn about the day-to-day realities.

**Step 5** – After the field trip, the whole group meets to share what they learned. A poll is taken to gauge how many students feel that they may have found a potential career path. Those who have discovered an interest are helped to develop a plan to learn more about that field or to find an internship.

Action research encourages learners to ask questions and arrive at conclusions that are based on data rather than uninformed opinions. It also shows them how to be proactive in pursuing their interests.

**Learning Conference** – A learning event in which students volunteer to make a presentation or demonstrate a skill in front of small groups of students. Picture a large room like a gymnasium, with six to ten tables. Learners are divided between the tables. Student presenters share their information to a small group. After 20 minutes, learners move to the next table to hear another peer presentation. Everyone rotates until they've been to all of the presentations. This is a great learning activity for older students to organize for younger learners.

*Facilitating in the Classroom*

## Engaging Lectures

Lectures will always be a vital part of the education process. Providing content is the right thing to do when:

- the topic is so complex or technical that it needs to be explained in detail or demonstrated
- the learners are so new to the topic that they need to be given basic information before they can play a meaningful role in the learning process
- there's an expert available who can share information and insights
- there's no other way for learners to engage with the materials other than through lectures

Lectures have major flaws, including that:

- they tend to turn learners into passive consumers
- they set the stage for distraction: young children fidget, older students check text messages or side chat
- the teacher often has no way of knowing if the material is meeting the needs of the learners, or if it's answering their main questions
- it places all of the responsibility for the effectiveness of the learning experience on the teacher

Happily, there are lots of ways to make lectures less passive and more engaging. Here are some relatively simple techniques to consider.

**The Participative Lecture** – Throughout your presentation, ask the group questions whenever you think that they'll be able to provide answers. After someone has made a comment, invite others to add their thoughts. Keep incorporating and building on student comments.

**Multiple Choice** – If you're using slides in your lecture, add a slide with a multiple-choice question or an open-ended question every few minutes. This encourages reflection and gets students talking. You can embed these questions using an app like *Slido.com*. If you don't have this technology, just open the floor for answers. Bounce ideas around to encourage dialogue.

**Fill in the Blanks** – Hand out a page or two of notes that summarize the material you're about to present, but leave blanks for key information. Place asterisks besides about 1/3 of the blanks and tell students that these items may be on an upcoming test. Students will understand that they need to listen to the whole lecture in order to fill the blank slots.

**Listening Teams** – Randomly hand out role cards. Place four roles in the deck: Questioners, Agreers, Nay-Sayers and Example Givers. Ask learners to listen to the lecture with their assigned role in mind. At the end of major points, invite comments from the four roles. Encourage students to debate each other.

*Chapter Seven: Learning Decisions*

**Group Questions** – Provide a brief overview of the lecture: objectives, topics to be covered, and issues to be explored. Invite learners to cluster around three or four pieces of flip chart paper posted around the room. Allow five minutes for the small groups to identify the questions, issues, and information they most want to take away from the lecture. Ask one person in each group to record the group comments. Invite groups to read out their questions before you resume your lecture. As you lecture, weave in answers to student questions. An alternative approach is to ask students to listen for the answers to their questions during the lecture. Then facilitate a discussion to hear their conclusions.

**Killer Question Contest Version #1** – Announce a group competition and prize for the dyad that creates the best test questions based on the lecture. This should be a question that challenges people to explore the topic more deeply. (Prizes can range from actual items, or extra privileges, to simply having one's name posted on an honor roll). Instruct everyone to listen to the lecture with the aim of figuring out the most challenging questions that could be asked to review the material. When your lecture is over, allow partners to *Brainstorm* and write down the two or three questions that they think meet the criteria. Facilitate a discussion to hear and record the best killer questions. Not every dyad will have a question to contribute, and there will be duplicates. Conduct a quick show of hands to see which killer questions people think are the best. Distribute these to small groups of three to four students. Allow ten to twenty minutes for discussion before you ask the groups to share their answers.

**Killer Question Contest Version # 2** – Ask each dyad to write their best killer question on an index card and then pass it to the pair sitting to the left of them. Immediately ask everyone to pass the question sheets one more time to the pair in front of them. Allow a few minutes while partners read the question they received. Invite students to read out any questions they don't fully understand so that you can clarify. Allow time for the partners to develop an answer to their question. Facilitate a plenary session to hear the answers. Record key points on the whiteboard or flip chart. Facilitate a discussion with

*Facilitating in the Classroom*

the whole class to discuss the best questions. To bring closure, hold a simple show of hands to identify the top killer question developed that day.

**So What?** – At the start of your lecture hand out blank index cards that feature the words *SO WHAT?* at the top of the page. Ask learners to listen to your lecture thinking about the ripple effects of the topic. This can be unintended consequences, other events that occurred as a result, people affected, etc. At the end of the lecture, form triads. Give these groups enough time to identify the ramifications and impacts arising from the topic. Facilitate a large group discussion to share student insights. If results need to be sorted, use one of the forms of *Multi-voting* described starting on page 59.

**The Envelope Please** – At the start of your lecture, hand out envelopes that were prepared ahead of time. Each envelope contains a sheet of paper with a single question. This is a question that will be raised or answered during your lecture. If you have a class of twenty students, try to have four or five different questions. Conduct your lecture. At the end, allow everyone time to record the answer to their question. Have them place their sheet into the envelope. Tell people to pass their envelopes until you say stop. Students open their new envelope, and read what the first person wrote. Allow time for students to add their comments. If time allows, pass the envelops along one more time. To bring closure, facilitate a large group discussion of the answers to the questions that you posed. Record answers if desired.

**Multiple-Hat Thinking** – Before the lecture, identify four to six roles that relate to the topic (e.g.: tenant farmer, merchant, tradesperson, soldier, landowner, etc.). Assign these roles randomly. More than one person can receive the same role. Instruct students to listen to the lecture as if they were that person. At the end of your presentation, facilitate a discussion about how specific stakeholders viewed the issue or situation. If time allows, create small groups composed of students assigned different hats to discuss the topic from different perspectives.

**Object Lesson** – This is about bringing objects that are related to the lesson into the classroom. These are physical items or pictures that have something to do with the lesson. If the class is young, you may need to supply the objects. Older students can be enrolled to round up the objects. At the start of the class, display all of the objects and pictures. At the end of your lecture, randomly distribute these items to small discussion groups of three to four students. Allow time for them to talk about how each item relates to the lecture. *"How is it connected?" "How was it used?" "Why does it matter?" "What does it tell us about the subject?"* End by facilitating a large-group sharing session.

**Planted Questions** – Create questions that relate to the topic. Write these on slips of paper and distribute them randomly, one per student. At the end of your lecture, form triads to discuss the best answer to the questions. Facilitate a large group discussion to share answers.

**Pick a Question** – Post topics around the room. These topics will be sub-sets of your lecture. Under each topic, post individual cards that feature specific questions. (You can have several cards that feature the same question.) Allow time for students to walk around to read all the cards. Then ask each person to pick a card and sit down. During your lecture, each student will make notes about their selected topic, in addition to making general notes. At the end of the lecture, you can either form small discussion groups of people who selected different questions, the same question, or facilitate a large group discussion to share various perspectives.

**Questions and Answers** – Buy index cards in two colors: blue and yellow, for example. Write questions related to the lecture topic on the blue cards (one question per card). Write answers to those same questions on the yellow cards (one answer per card). Shuffle the two decks separately. Give each student one blue card and one yellow card. After the lecture invite students to mingle to find the answer to their question. Set a strict time limit. Learners should end up with two cards representing their original blue question card and the related yellow answer card. Facilitate a discussion to hear the questions and answers.

**Tossed Salad** – Place a large plastic bowl on a table in the middle of the room. Distribute small slips of paper and challenge learners to write down the single most important issue or question they have about the subject of the lecture. They can write that question right away, or wait until they hear your talk. Conduct the lecture. About twenty minutes before the end of the session, ask everyone to fold their question slip and drop them into the bowl. Ask someone to toss the questions. Pass the bowl around the room so everyone can take one, or scoop out handfuls of questions and distribute them. Form small, four-person discussion groups. Ask groups to quickly read all of the questions they received, and then discuss the one or two that they think are most significant. Facilitate a large group discussion to share insights.

*Facilitating in the Classroom*

**You're Next** – Design your presentation so that there's a question for students to answer every five to ten minutes. If you're using slides, integrate question slides into the slide pack. Place a large plastic bowl near the front of the room. Distribute paper slips and ask learners to write their first and last names on their slip. Ask students to fold their slips in quarters then collect them. Place the folded slips in the bowl. Toss the slips to mix them. Start your presentation. When you come to one of the question slides, give the group a few minutes to think about the answer. Ask someone to pull a slip from the bowl and read the name. That person is challenged to answer the question. If they succeed, great. If that student is unable to answer the question, invite others to respond. Keep going until someone gets it right. Whoever succeeds, draws the next name from the bowl. You can bring the bowl back over a series of classes until every name has been drawn.

**Color Cards** – Give each student a set of five cards. Explain when it's appropriate for them to raise one of the cards. Caution them against overusing the cards, as this can be disruptive. Below is just one suggestion for the cards. You can, of course, create other criteria.

> **Black** – I have something important/relevant to share about what we're discussing.
> **Red** – I have an important observation about the process e.g.: the discussion has gone off track, we need more time, etc.
> **Orange** – I have a question about the content.
> **Yellow** – I have a question about the process.
> **Green** – I'd like to ask another student a question.

**Response Cards** – Distribute blank index cards. Create categories and invite people to record ideas on their cards as the lecture unfolds. Make sure that people write the category title on each index card. Here are some possible categories:

1. A question about the subject of the session is…
2. A solution to a problem being discussed is….
3. An expectation or need about this topic is….
4. A fact that has not been mentioned yet is….
5. A hypothesis I've formed about the subject is…

At the end of the lecture, use the response cards a number of ways. The simplest is to facilitate a large group discussion to share the most significant comments and questions people wrote on their cards. Another option is to form triads to hold these discussions, then invite people to share highlights with the whole class.

**Stop and Focus** – Design a lecture to feature a short preamble. This is an introduction to the topic that includes the objectives of the lecture, the topics to be covered, and the ideas you plan to share. Invite everyone to find a partner. Allow dyads five minutes to identify what they most want to learn about the topic. You could make this more concrete by asking: *"If this lecture clarifies only one thing really thoroughly, what would that be?"* or *"If this lecture answers only one question for you, what is it?"* Allow partners five minutes to discuss their individual objectives or questions. Partners don't need to agree. Facilitate a discussion to hear some of the questions. You don't need to get one from each person, as there will be duplicates. Record the main points of interest on a flip chart or whiteboard. You can use a quick show of hands to find out which topics interest the greatest number of people. Proceed with your lecture knowing which topics to highlight.

**Mid-point Check** – Stop in the middle of the lecture, and announce that you're taking a group pulse. Invite a show of hands in response to questions about the process. Some areas to check: Pace of the lecture: *"Is it too fast/too slow?"* Depth of the content: *"Is it too deep/just right/too shallow?"* Focus: *"Is anyone lost? Does anyone need to go back? Do any points need further clarification?"*

If you want to use an app like *pollanywhere.com* for this you will need to have students to download that app in advance of the class. You will also need to upload the survey to the polling site. This calls for preparation, but gets instant results and ensures anonymity.

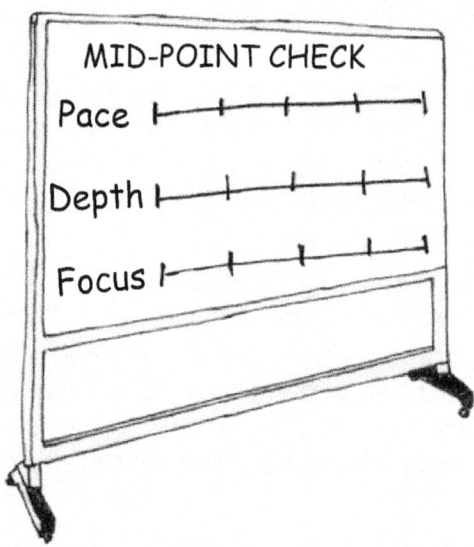

**Color Groups** – Identify four to six themes within your presentation. Post these themes around the room. Link each theme to a color. Assign each student a color by distributing blank colored cards. During the lecture, each student pays attention to the aspect of the lecture that's linked to their assigned color. At the end of the lecture, invite learners to form themselves into small groups. Each group must have members with different color cards. Allow fifteen to twenty minutes for small groups to share their observations. End by facilitating a discussion of the whole group to hear small group insights.

*Facilitating in the Classroom*

**Talk Circuit** – Post a few key questions at the start of your lecture. Tell students that they will have an opportunity to answer those questions at the end of your presentation. Twenty minutes before the end of the class, ask each person to find a partner. It adds energy if you get them all to stand somewhere in the room as if they were at a party. Give partners only three to four minutes to discuss one or more of the questions. When the time is up, ask each person to find a second partner to share their original thoughts plus any ideas that they picked from their last partner. Repeat as often as time allows. End by facilitating a large group discussion.

**Structured Observation** – Before the class, create a structured observation sheet. For example, for class about effective presentation skills, create a list of the traits shared by all excellent presentations. Give a brief overview about each trait listed on the sheet. Ask learners to pay attention to this checklist of best practices, while they listen to presentations by fellow students. At the end of each presentation, invite observers to provide feedback about what the presenter did well, and what they could do to become even better. (Do not allow anyone to mention what was not done well, only what could be done to improve).

**Test Challenge Teams** – At the start of a term, form test teams of four to five students. Assign the teams the task of creating the perfect test: one that will stump the other teams. Distribute sample test questions to help students understand the format. Limit test questions to four. At the end of the term, stage a test competition. Create a test ladder. When you hold the competition invite teams to sit in chairs at the front of the room. The team asking their questions reads out one at a time. The team members being tested can confer before they answer. Set a timer that rings when time is up. Keep track of scores on a scoreboard. If there's a tie, hold a tiebreaker with questions that you created. Reward the winning team.

**Headlines** – Before you start the lecture, challenge students to come up with the best one-liner to summarize the topic. Hand out markers and long strips of flip chart paper. At the end of the lecture, allow a few minutes while everyone writes a pithy, poignant, or funny headline that captures the essence of the lesson. Invite students hold up their headlines one at a time and read them out. Discuss the ones that get a big reaction.

**Video Production** – Since so many classes are being taught online, internet discussion groups have become more common. In addition to exchanging written comments on a group site, groups can share videos. One possible activity is to ask each student to record a three-to-four-minute video at the end of a term or topic. This is either a short summary of what they learned, or a commentary about a significant part of the content.

## Managing Time

Keeping small groups on schedule is always a challenge. It's very common for some groups to finish fast, while others beg for more time. Below are some strategies to keep a class on track:

- Post the activity parameters and timeframes for each activity. If a lesson has steps or stages, post allotted times for each segment.
- Read all of the guidelines aloud before turning learners loose. Check for comprehension. Ask randomly selected students to repeat the instructions. Ask if anyone has a question.
- Walk around and monitor progress. Are students getting stuck or going off on a tangent? Are they working within the timeframe?
- Periodically check in to see if groups have any questions about the process.
- If a group finishes early, give them a bonus question to consider, or an extra activity to complete. Prepare these activities and questions in advance. Either hand these out, or train students to automatically pick up a bonus question from the front of the room in case they finish early.
- Place a countdown timer in clear sight and call out key time markers.
- A few minutes before the end of the session, ask groups to start wrapping up.

## Sharing Group Learning

Many participative learning activities feature venues for sharing, known as plenaries. When students are asked to present what they've learned, it challenges them to organize their thoughts into coherent and succinct ideas. These sharing sessions turn students into teachers, and allow classmates to benefit from a variety of perspective.

The teacher's role during plenary sessions is to act as the neutral facilitator who orchestrates the debriefing, without interjecting too much content. Below are some optional ways to conduct plenary sessions.

*Facilitating in the Classroom*

**Plenary Sessions**

When you divide a class into small discussion groups, it's a common practice to bring them together at the end to share their answers. Large group sharing is especially beneficial if each of the small groups focused on different aspects of the same problem or topic.

Plenaries do, however, have a downside; they can be time consuming and quickly become boring if several groups repeat similar points. With these issues in mind, here are some ways to manage large group sharing sessions:

**Option #1 – Group Presentations.** This is the most straightforward approach. Simply work your way around the room, allowing each group to present their findings or conclusions for a predetermined amount of time.

> **Pros**: Each group gets their moment in the spotlight. Everyone gets to benefit from the insights of others. The teacher has the opportunity to assess the quality and completeness of the information generated by the students. The teacher can identify knowledge gaps that need to be filled with lectures.

> **Cons**: It can take forever, and become tiresome if too many groups make similar points. Some groups will take too long. Later groups may find that their points have already been covered. People tune out when it takes too long, or if it gets repetitious.

**Option # 2 – Prioritize Findings.** At the end of the small group discussions, hand out voting dots or markers. Using one of the *Multi-voting* techniques described starting on page 59. Instruct each group to rank their ideas. Clarify the voting criteria. This could be most important, most innovative, easiest to implement, etc. Once each group has tabulated their votes, work your way around the room recording only the top ranked ideas from each group. Then go around again and record the second ranked idea in each group, and so on.

> **Pros**: No need to hear everything that each group discussed; only the key ideas. It's faster. Every group is heard from sooner. No one goes last or gets totally preempted.

> **Cons:** Only works if all the small groups were working on the same overarching topic, in which case, the summary may feel somewhat out of context.

**Option # 3 – Gallery Walk.** Ask each group to make clear and concise notes about their main findings on a piece of flip chart paper. Place these sheets as far apart as possible. Invite learners to walk from chart to chart reading the findings of each group, as if they were looking at art. If the small groups had facilitators, ask them to stay behind to explain their group's findings to each new set of visitors. Use a timer and announce whenever it's time for groups to move to the next flip chart.

**Pros:** Everyone is up and moving around which creates energy. Every group has the opportunity to share their findings.

**Cons:** If facilitators weren't used, visitors may not fully understand the notes. If there were facilitators, they will be stuck repeating their presentation, while also missing out on what was learned in other groups.

You can end a *Gallery Walk* by facilitating a discussion in the large group to share one or two highlights from each small group. Ask one student from each group to present their highlight.

**Idea Boards**

Another way to share small group ideas is to create idea boards. Find an empty wall. Create separate sections for each topic. At the end of small group discussions, hand out index cards and tape. Ask each group to post bullet-point summaries and drawings of their findings. Learners walk around to review each other's work. Once learners have read all of the notes, ask them to return to their seats. Ask one person from each team to give a short overview of what they discovered. After these presentations, the teacher presents a lecture to build on the students' discoveries, and to offer additional insights.

**Video Presentations** - Instead of making presentations in the classroom, learners can create and share videos. One possible activity is to ask each student to record a three- to four-minute video that summarizes an activity or experiment. This can either be a short summary of what was learned, or a commentary about a significant insight.

Engagement strategies like the ones described in this chapter benefit not only students, but teachers too. Teachers get a better understanding of the learning needs and interests of their students. They also receive feedback that enables them to fine tune future lectures. Moreover, they play a key role in creating an energetic, inclusive and engaging classroom experience.

*Facilitating in the Classroom*

# Chapter Eight: Structured Conversations

Facilitators always plan every meeting in step-by-step detail. This helps them determine how to organize the participants, how much time to allocate for each segment of the activity, and which supplies will be needed. Teachers who are planning participative classroom activities will also need to do this. To arm you with more techniques for structuring your next class, this chapter will:

- describe an array of process tools that provide much needed structure to complex conversations
- suggest a variety of ways to use process tools in different subject areas

There are scores of structured conversations out there. Since only a few can be mentioned in this book, please refer to the annotated bibliography on page 133 for suggestions about where you can find additional templates.

## Structured Conversation # 1: Sequential Questioning

One of the best ways to encourage students to drill deeply into a subject is to pose a series of prepared questions. These questions should be graduated from macro to micro: start at 30,000 feet and work down to ground level. Note that the questions are a combination of both open- and close-ended.

In this activity, students write their names on slips of paper that are tossed into a bowl at the front of the room. Names are drawn from the bowl to determine who will answer the next question. After each turn, the student who answered the previous question gets to pick the name of the next contestant. This creates a game show atmosphere that's ideal for winding down the week.

**Steps in the process:**

**Step 1:** Select your topic. This should be a topic that has a lot of complexity and will elicit lots of opinions. Create eight to twelve questions that will make students think deeply about the subject. Structure the questions to go from big picture to personal impact. The example that follows will help you understand the format.

**Step 2**: Write each question at the top of its own sheet of flip chart paper. Leave the rest of that sheet blank to allow room to record group observations. Only let students see one question at a time. If you use a whiteboard, do not write a question until you're ready to reveal it.

**Step 3:** Pose the first question. Allow a few minutes of thinking time. Ask someone to pick a name out of the bowl. That student gets the first attempt to answer the question. While they respond, stay neutral, paraphrase their comments, and ask probing questions to get them to dig deeper. Record the student's response, then invite others to add their perspective. Facilitate a conversation so that everyone is engaged. Record all comments. If people disagree, simply note that these are differing points of view. You will be able to add more information and sort right from wrong at the end of the activity.

**Step 4:** Move to the next question. Allow a few minutes so that everyone can think of an answer. Then invite the person who answered the previous question to pick a name out of the bowl. The person whose name was drawn will answer next. Repeat until all of the questions have been answered.

**Step 5:** Go back through the answers to add information that was missed, or to correct any mistaken ideas.

## Sequential Questioning Example

**Topic:** The Internet is a major factor in the economy, the country and in our personal lives.

> **Question 1:** The Internet is the single most significant innovation of the 20$^{th}$ century. Yes or no? Explain your answer.
>
> **Question 2:** No business can survive today without shifting a major portion of their enterprise online. Yes or no? Explain your answer.
>
> **Question 3:** While there are some drawbacks to the Internet, it's been an overwhelmingly positive asset, and a force for good. Yes or no? Explain your answer.
>
> **Question 4:** How has the Internet changed the way people get their news? Is this good or bad?
>
> **Question 5:** What are the best things about being connected to the World-Wide Web that enables communication all over the globe?
>
> **Question 6:** What are the worst things about being connected to the World Wide Web that enables communication all over the globe?
>
> **Question 7:** If there was one thing about the impact of the Internet that you could change, what would it be?
>
> **Question 8:** Based on your personal experience, what one piece of advice would you give to young people just starting to use social media?

Sequential Questioning looks like a rather simple activity, but looks are deceiving. This process engages students in drilling down on an issue. It also teaches them to hear and appreciate different perspectives. Once you use this dynamic process, you'll find many applications.

*Facilitating in the Classroom*

## Structured Conversation #2: Constructive Controversy

This is a very different way to structure a debate. In a conventional debate, teams compete to win an argument. The focus of this classic form of debating is to negate the views of the other party. In *Constructive Controversy*, the emphasis is on listening and appreciating what the other party is saying.

*Constructive Controversy* helps ensure that everyone really listens to differing points of view. It also encourages students to draw conclusions based on evidence and well-structured reasoning. Use it when there are two or more opposing ideas inherent in a topic, and when exploration of these differences has the potential to yield important insights. This process is also a helpful method for healing a rift between two parties.

**Steps in the Process**

**Step 1:** Select a topic that features differing points of view. Form two advocacy teams and allow sufficient time for preparation.

**Step 2:** Review the *Norms* for healthy debates on page 73. Post these, and inform the class that you will intervene when any of the rules are violated.

**Step 3:** Seat the two advocacy teams at the front of the room. Set a timer. Allow the first team to present its case to the class. Members of the opposing advocacy teams are told to take notes and ask probing questions that push the first team to defend their position. No one is allowed to argue or refute ideas. Allow the second team to present their case in a repeat of the process above.

**Step 4:** After both teams have presented their main arguments, allow time for teams to have a huddle to review the best points made by the other teams. They are then challenged to use these points to create a new presentation that completely reverses their original positions. Stated another way, advocacy teams are to construct a new argument that's directly counter to their first position. This exploration drives teams to gain new insights.

**Step 5:** Teams take turns presenting their newly crafted counter-positions to the wider group. Once again, observers can only ask probing questions.

**Step 6:** When all of the advocacy presentations are complete, invite students to share their most significant revelations about how the debate reshaped their opinions. Ask them what they learned from totally reversing their point of view? Record these insights on a flip chart or whiteboard. You can stop here or add the next step.

**Step 7:** Ask students to drop their advocacy roles to have a large group decision. Record the main arguments that were presented by the teams. Give members voting dots or markers. Invite team members to come to the flip chart or whiteboard to vote for the most significant arguments made.

Students can place all of their dots on a single idea, or divide their dots in a way that reflects which ideas they found to be most important. Tally the votes and ratify the choice with the members. This will give you a snapshot of what was most significant.

Constructive Controversy teaches people to listen carefully to the views of others. It develops empathy and demonstrates how an open attitude leads to greater insight. It also highlights the fact that there's always more than one way to look at any situation.

## Constructive Controversy Topics

This process can be used to explore just about any topic in which there are two points of view. Here are a few examples:

- The government should subsidize renewable forms of energy.
- Human beings should fund a space mission to Mars.
- Social media comments should be protected by freedom of speech.
- Video games are too violent.
- It is never appropriate for government to restrict freedom of speech.
- The voting age should be lowered.
- The driving age should be raised.
- America should not give foreign aid to other countries.
- People should be fined for not voting.
- Sports stars make too much money.
- The death penalty should be abolished.
- Everyone should be a vegetarian.
- All students should be required to have an after-school job.
- School uniforms should be mandatory.
- Schools should punish cyber-bullying that happens outside of school.
- Schools should block YouTube.
- Year-round education is better for students.
- Homework should be banned.
- Education is the key to future success.

*Facilitating in the Classroom*

## Structured Conversation #3: *SWOT Analysis*

This is an analysis tool useful to identify all of the competing elements in a situation. The letters stand for Strengths, Weaknesses, Opportunities, and Threats. *SWOT Analysis is* very useful for analyzing situations that feature complex variables. It is most commonly used to help groups decide whether or not to pursue a particular course of action.

*SWOT Analysis* creates a balanced picture of both the internal and external factors at play in a situation. It teaches learners that there are often more complexities present than were first understood.

Before students can complete in a *SWOT Analysis*, they have to do their homework. One approach might be to start the analysis so that students can figure out where they have knowledge gaps. They can then conduct focused research and complete the analysis when they have sufficient information.

**Steps in the Process**

**Step 1**: Clarify the topic to be discussed. Circulate questions associated with the four categories of inquiry well in advance so that students have time to prepare. A set of common *SWOT* questions is provided on the next page, although these may not fit all situations. On a whiteboard or pair of flip chart sheets, draw the diagram shown below:

**Step 2:** Facilitate a discussion in which students share their responses to the questions. This is not a decision-making conversation, so you should record all comments, including opposing views. If the class has more than 20 students, create sub-groups of four to five students. Give each group their own **SWOT** graph. Ask each group to appoint someone to record ideas. Allow 15 - 20 minutes for small groups to discuss and record their responses. Conduct a plenary to share each group's analysis.

*Chapter Eight: Structured Conversations*

**Step 3**: Hand out voting dots or markers, and invite learners to mark the three items they think are most important in each section of the graph. If you used small groups, have them *Multi-vote* on their group chart first, then start a new *SWOT* summary chart that combines that top-rated items from each subgroup.

**Step 4:** Bring closure by connecting the results of the *SWOT Analysis*. If the chart is about a historical event, help students to discussion how the information surfaced by the *SWOT Analysis* might have altered past decision making. If the students analyzed a current challenge, help them identify any action steps that the *SWOT Analysis* is suggesting.

## Sample *SWOT* Questions

**Strengths:**
- What do we do really well?
- What are our greatest assets?
- What are we most proud of having accomplished?
- What makes us unique?
- What special skills or talents have we got?
- What are some of our greatest past successes?

**Weaknesses:**
- What don't we do well?
- What are our greatest liabilities?
- In what areas do we tend to underperform?
- What are our limitations in the areas of resources, teamwork, technology, access to research data, etc?
- What skills or resources do we lack on our team?
- What are our limitations as a team?
- Why haven't we fixed these limitations?

**Opportunities:**
- What trends or new ideas could we incorporate?
- What are others asking us to do differently?
- What synergies can we create with other groups?
- How can we turn some of our weaknesses or threats into opportunities?
- What could we do differently?

**Threats:**
- What's the biggest potential mistake to make in this venture?
- Who is our biggest competitor/opponent in this venture?
- What could they do to harm us/our project?
- What's the worst thing that we could do?
- What threat have we underestimated or failed to consider?
- What threats do our weaknesses expose us to?

## SWOT Analysis Examples:

This four-quadrant analysis tool can be applied to both macro- or micro-issues. You can use it to help assess a current challenge, or to go back and explore an event in history.

- The winter invasion of Russia by Napoleon's army.
- The battle strategies of the Third Reich.
- Rome's ability to control a far-flung empire.
- American interventions to bring peace to the Middle East.
- Bringing Internet services to rural areas.
- The mission to colonize Mars.
- A winning season for our school's football team.

*SWOT Analysis* encourages people to see all aspects of a situation before they plunge into action. Once a *SWOT* analysis is complete, people are better able to plan strategies that deal with a variety of possible scenarios. They also have information that allows them to better assess whether or not a past activity was properly addressed.

*Chapter Eight: Structured Conversations*

## Structured Conversation #4: *Brainstorming*

*Brainstorming* is the most widely known facilitation tool. It was created to generate numerous ideas quickly. The unique feature of this process is that all ideas are accepted. This non-judgmental approach encourages everyone to speak up.

You can *Brainstorm* just about anything. Use it at the start of a lesson to create a list of possible topics to explore. *Brainstorm* to generate a list of potential solutions to a problem. Use it and the end of a lesson to generate a rapid-fire summary key points raised by a specific lesson.

**Steps in the Process**

**Step 1:** Clarify the topic or problem for which you need ideas. Allow quiet time while people think.

**Step 2:** Review the rules of *Brainstorming*:

- Let ideas flow
- Be creative
- Build on other's ideas
- Keep it moving

-There are no bad ideas
-Think in new ways
- Break out of old patterns
- No judging or critiquing

**Step 3:** Facilitate a non-decision-making conversation in which you invite everyone to just shout out their ideas. Encourage people to keep it coming as fast as possible. Avoid going round-robin to keep it spontaneous. Record ideas quickly as they come up without discussing or questioning them.

**Step 4:** At some point, the pace will slow. When all of the obvious ideas have been suggested, keep things moving by asking probing questions. This encourages people to dig deeper. Some typical questions include:

"What if money were no object?"
"What would you do if we were in charge of the school?"
"What would no one expect us to do?"
"What's something that we've never done before?"

**Step 6:** When the flow of ideas appears to have totally stopped, go back and explore each suggestion in some detail, so that each idea is fully developed and clearly understood. Combine similar thoughts to eliminate duplicates.

**Step 7:** Use one of the forms of *Multi-voting* methods described starting on page 59 to identify the most viable ideas.

*Facilitating in the Classroom*

# Structured Conversation #5: Affinity Diagrams

This is a useful tool for organizing a large amount of random information into coherent themes. It gets people up and moving, and makes random ideas more manageable. Since it's a graphic tool, you'll need a large wall space.

**Steps in the Process**

**Step 1**: Clarify the topic being discussed. This can be a historical event that's being analyzed, a book that's being reviewed, or a problem that's being solved.

**Step 2**: Clear a large section of whiteboard or wall space. Invite the class to help identify the headings or categories that will be explored. Categories will vary from topic to topic. Write each header on a sheet and post it as shown below:

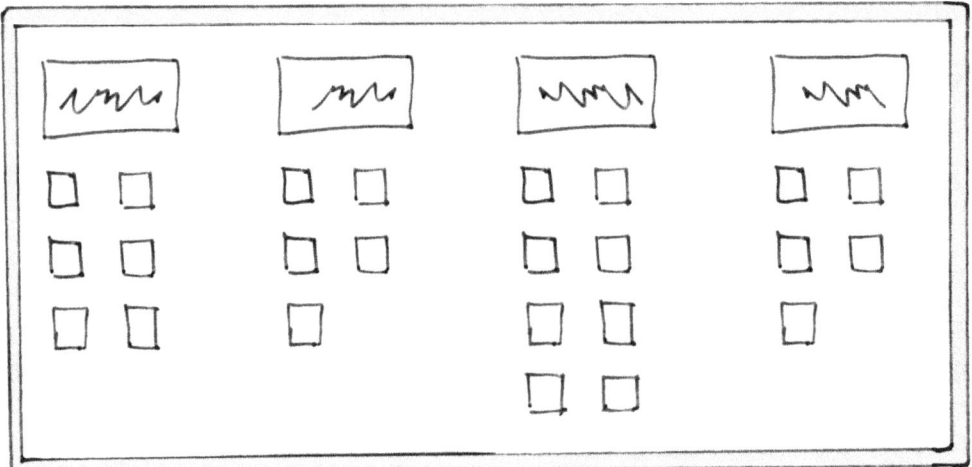

**Step 3**: At the end of small group discussions, ask students to write their ideas on blank paper or sticky notes. Go around the class and invite students to read out the ideas they've recorded. After all ideas have been read aloud, allow more quiet time during which people can write any additional thoughts that come to mind.

**Step 4**: Invite everyone to approach the *Affinity Diagram* to post their idea cards in the categories where they fit. Clarify the placement of any ideas that may be unclear or seem to fit in two places.

**Step 5:** Review how ideas are organized. Stick duplicate ideas over one another. Ask learners questions like: *"Which categories have the most ideas?" "What does that tell us about the situation or problem?" "Why were there so few ideas in some of the other areas?"* Facilitate a discussion to discover more suggestions.

**Step 6:** Rank the ideas by handing out markers or *Multi-voting* dots. Allow students to pick the three most significant items in each topic area. Review the top picks and ratify the results.

*Chapter Eight: Structured Conversations*

## Structured Conversation #6: *Forcefield* Analysis

This is a structured method of looking at the two opposing forces at play in a situation. Useful when you need to surface all of the barriers and problems that could hamper progress. *Forcefield Analysis* also helps to clarify the strengths and resources that can be deployed. *Forcefield Analysis* helps ensure that assessments are balanced and thorough.

**Steps in the Process**

**Step 1:** Clarify the topic, situation or project to be analyzed.

**Step 2:** Draw a line down the center of a sheet of flip chart paper or section of whiteboard. Mark the two forces as shown in the diagram below.

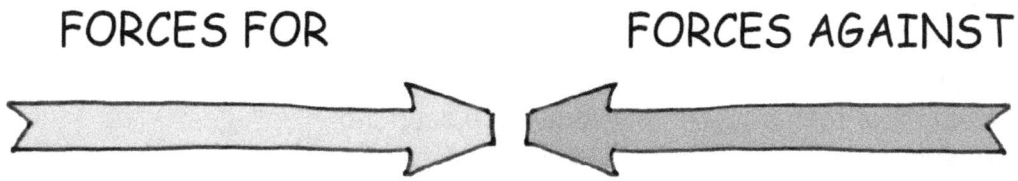

**Step 3**: Facilitate a discussion to generate a list of factors under each heading. Start with the positives, then move on to the negatives.

---

**Sample Topic:**
**Forces working for and against us winning next month's science fair**

| What's working for us? | What's working against us? |
|---|---|
| • talented, hardworking team | • coordinating everybody's time |
| • state-of-the-art computers | • no one artistic on the team |
| • a great teacher | • difficulty getting raw materials |
| • a great room to work in | • not enough time during the week to complete all the tasks |

*Facilitating in the Classroom*

**Step 4:** Provide learners with markers. Invite them to come up to the completed *Forcefield* chart to place their checkmarks beside the three most important factors on both lists. Remind them that they can't place more than one check mark on a single item.

**Step 5:** Tally the marks to arrive at a ranking of both the positives and the negatives. Facilitate a discussion of how the team can leverage the positives as well as overcome the negatives.

## Variations of *Forcefield* Analysis

*Forcefield* Analysis has other variations helpful for examining any problem or situation from different perspectives. These variations include:

| ✓ **Pros** | × **Cons** |
|---|---|
| ✓ Things we're doing well | × Things we could do better |
| ✓ Hopes | × Fears |
| ✓ Best case scenario | × Worst case scenario |
| ✓ Assets | × Liabilities |
| ✓ Strengths | × Weaknesses |
| ✓ Positives | × Negatives |
| ✓ Opportunities | × Obstacles |

*Examples:*     **Forces for**     **Forces against**

- Britain's ability to hold onto the American colonies
- Reducing the influence of lobbyists and big donors
- Eliminating single-use plastics
- Eliminating coins and paper money
- Maintaining freedom of speech

*Examples:*     ***Pros***     ***Cons***

- Mandatory voting
- Access to social media by children under twelve
- Raising the drinking age
- Expanding the Supreme Court
- Mandatory school uniforms
- Twelve month school year

# Structured Conversation #7: Decision Grid

When you have a list of ideas that require sorting, it can be very effective to use a grid. This is especially true if the ideas being sorted are complex. A decision grid allows you to compare more than one option against a set of criteria. This tends to make the decision-making process both thorough and objective.

Grids can turn random and polarized debates into objective assessments. Since everyone has an opportunity to express opinions and cast votes, buy-in for the outcome is high. The most common type of decision grid has a set of criteria.

## Steps in the Process

**Step 1:** Identify the options you need to sort. The ideal number is from three to six.

**Step 2:** Invite students to *Brainstorm* all of the possible criteria against which options could be judged. Some common criteria include:

- saves time
- saves money
- reduces stress
- is timely
- is feasible
- supports our strategic goal
- is something we can control
- includes the most people
- is affordable
- is fun

**Step 3:** Review the criteria, then use a form of *Multi-voting* to determine which criteria will be used. Tally the votes to identify the criteria to be used. The criteria are placed along the top of the grid. The options being considered are placed on the vertical side. Create a chart like the one shown below:

| OPTION | COST | COMPLEXITY | TIMELINESS | INNOVATION | TOTALS |
|---|---|---|---|---|---|
| A | 1 1 1 1 | 2 3 3 2 | 3 3 3 3 | 4 4 3 4 | 43 |
| B | 1 2 1 1 | 3 4 3 3 | 3 4 3 4 | 4 4 3 3 | 45 |
| C | 1 2 2 1 | 3 3 4 3 | 3 3 4 4 | 3 4 3 3 | 46 |

*Facilitating in the Classroom*

**Step 4:** Before students vote, explain the system for weighting the votes. Invite students to come to the board to rate how well each option meets the criteria. Use the scale below.

> *(x 1) = does not meet the criteria*
> *(x 2) = somewhat meets the criteria*
> *(x 3) = good at meeting the criteria*

**Step 5:** Ask someone to tally the weighted votes. Discuss and ratify the final choice.

*Criteria-Based Decision Grids* take some time to construct and deploy, so these should be reserved for situations that are both complex and important. When the options are clearly understood, and when people get a chance to share their thinking before they vote, the results are viewed by all as fair and objective.

*Chapter Eight: Structured Conversations*

## Structured Conversation #8: Surveys

To gather feedback, facilitators create a quick survey with four or five simple questions. They post the survey and invite group members to give their ratings. Surveys can be used in the middle of a lesson to determine if things are on track, or at the end of a lesson to gauge group opinion.

### Steps in the Process

**Step 1:** Clarify the subject of the survey. Create the survey on a sheet of flip chart paper or on a whiteboard. Create from three to six questions, as per the example shown.

**Step 2:** Post the survey and provide markers so that learners can rate each item. If anonymity is important, hand out adhesive dots and invite students to mark each dot with both the number of the question and their rating. Collect all the dots and post them.

**Step 3:** Facilitate a discussion about the results, by asking: *"What do these ratings tell us? What changes can we make to improve any of the low ratings?"*

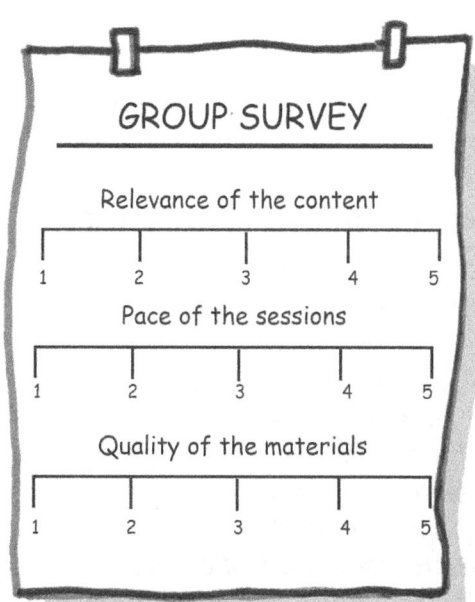

Surveys can provide a snapshot of group opinion or identify problem areas that need to be addressed. Surveys are simple to use and people love to take them because they're usually curious about how others have rated the same situation.

*Facilitating in the Classroom*

## Structured Conversation #9: Systematic Problem Solving

On occasion, you may need to explore an issue in depth. This might be a real-world problem faced by the school, or the community, or it might be about an academic topic.

When problems are solved without structure, People tend to blurt out solutions as soon as a problem is named. The whole group will then move off in pursuit of that idea, or start to argue. The other issue with this approach is that solutions were suggested before the current situation was properly assessed.

*Systematic Problem Solving* was created to deal with this tendency. This process involves taking the time to first understand the problem situation: to analyze it in depth before jumping to conclusions.

Once a problem has been fully analyzed, then, and only then, are solutions sought. The best way to do this is to use *Brainstorming* since it encourages the development of a wide range of potential solutions. Since no one judges or criticizes ideas, they tend to flow. The result is greater creativity and innovation.

### Steps in the Process

**Step 1:** Define the problem or issue to ensure that everyone is clear about exactly what is being discussed.

**Step 2:** Analyze the problem by asking probing questions. This encourages people to think analytically. The object here is to dig down to get to the underlying root-causes.

Questions facilitators commonly ask:

- *Describe this problem to me in step-by-step detail.*
- *What is it? How does it manifest itself?*
- *What are the noticeable signs of it?*
- *What makes this happen?*
- *How are people affected?*
- *What other problems does it cause?*
- *What are the most damaging aspects?*
- *What stops us from solving it?*
- *Who gets in the way of solving it?*
- *What's the root cause of each symptom? (5 Whys)*

**Step 3:** Once the problem has been fully analyzed, facilitate a discussion to identify potential solutions. Use *Brainstorming* to generate potential solutions. The steps of *Brainstorming* are on page 119.

**Step 4:** Use either *Multi-voting* (page 59) or a decision grid (page 123) to determine which of the *Brainstormed* ideas ought to be pursued.

**Step 5:** Summarize the results of the problem-solving exercise by discussing the solution or solutions proposed by the group. If these solutions are going to be implemented, help the students develop action plans that specify what will be done, how, by when, and by whom.

*Systematic Problem Solving* provides a structured and disciplined way to explore a complex and important issue. It eliminates the tendency for people to make snap judgments and ensures that the whole group is engaged at every step. This results in a sense of real consensus about the outcome.

## Sample Problem Solving Topics

There are endless subject areas that lend themselves to problem solving from history to political science, from social studies to current events.

Students can also use this multi-step process to tackle problems that they're encountering on school projects. Below are a few examples of problems that lend themselves to *Systematic Problem Solving*:

- The digital divide.
- Resistance to *Going Green*.
- Low graduation rates in urban areas.
- Lack of intercultural communication.
- Wasting time playing video games.
- Poor childhood food choices.
- Youth who feel and act entitled.
- Cyberbullying.
- Too few girls in science and math.
- Starting over at a new school.
- The intrusion of technology in our lives.
- Intrusive safety and security measures.
- Low rates of voter turnout.
- Low turnout at school social events.

*Facilitating in the Classroom*

# Enhance Your Facilitation Skills

The best way to improve your skills in front of groups is to take a Facilitation Skills Workshop. If you have the time and money, consider attending a facilitation skills workshop that features practice rounds and observer feedback. Providers vary by geography, but can easily be found by conducting an online search for either *Facilitator Training* or *Facilitation Skills Workshops.* This is absolutely the best way to accelerate your learning curve.

**Enroll in an Online Facilitation Skills Course**

If you can't spare the time to attend a workshop, there is an online option available through our website. This is the only online course on the subject of facilitation skills in existence. This course isn't the usual boring set of slides you get with most online courses. Our program features forty-seven video clips showing both the right and the wrong way to facilitate. There's a test at the end of the course. which results in a certificate of completion. The cost for six months of unlimited access is $99.00 for a single enrollment, with discounts for groups going as low as $15.00 per person.

View the program outline on the next page.
Preview a lesson on our website.
**www.facilitationtutor.com**
Send an email to obtain a free preview enrollment.
Ingrid@facilitationtutor.com

# The Facilitation Skills Online Program   (3 to 5 hours viewing time)

- The program is organized into ten lessons.
- Each lesson isolates a single, important technique.
- Each core skill is demonstrated in a group setting.
- Theoretical models are clearly and simply explained.
- Interactive exercises and structured practice activities accompany each lesson.
- Each lesson is supported by downloadable workbook pages.
- The program is linked to an online bookstore, featuring recommended further reading.
- A final test allows learners to receive a Certificate of Completion.

### Lesson 1 – Introduction to Facilitation

- introduces the concept of facilitation: its purpose and underlying beliefs
- provides an overview of the foundational content/process model
- clarifies misunderstanding about facilitator assertiveness
- examines how leaders can balance facilitating with being directive.

### Lesson 2 – The Five Core Practices

- describes the five core practices of facilitation
- demonstrates the five core practices in action
- explores the boundaries of neutrality
- recommends ways to use the five core practices in various settings.

### Lesson 3 – The Start Sequence

- provides a clear structure for beginning any facilitated session
- offers examples of start sequences of varying complexity
- shows how the start sequence can be used to maintain focus throughout any facilitated session.

### Lesson 4 – Establishing *Norms*

- explores the challenging situations that occur in meetings
- shows how *Norming* can create and maintain a positive meeting climate
- demonstrates how targeted *Norming* can be used to deal with difficult situations.

### Lesson 5 – Recording Group Ideas

- describes the purpose and importance of flip-chart note taking
- creates awareness of both the best and worst practices of recording group ideas
- describes the rules of wording and demonstrates them in action.

*Facilitating in the Classroom*

### Lesson 6 – Conflict Intervention Techniques

- emphasizes the importance of assertively managing conflict in groups
- provides a technique for intervening to redirect member behaviors
- shares a specific model for addressing group conflict that is both non-confrontational and effective
- provides guidance for getting through those difficult moments in any meeting.

### Lesson 7 – Process Checking

- explores the hidden reasons that meetings falter
- provides a specific set of steps for taking the pulse and restoring group effectiveness
- shares techniques for conducting written process checks.

### Lesson 8 – Conversation Structure

- describes the two categories of conversations
- provides strategies for the two types of conversations to manage complex decision-making discussions
- offers specific strategies for managing the dynamic shift between these two modes.

### Lesson 9 – Decision-Making Tools

- outlines the various ways that groups can make decisions and clarify whether they unite or divide group members
- demonstrates situations in which each approach is applicable
- illustrates how various decision-making tools can be used in combination to arrive at solutions everyone can live with.

### Lesson 10 – Ending a Facilitation

- provides a checklist of what facilitators do to effectively end facilitated discussions
- demonstrates a variety of ways to bring closure
- provides tools for overcoming blocks to consensus
- provides a format for action planning
- shares strategies to avoid poor follow-through.

---

Prices for the online course range from $99.00 for a single enrollment to $15.00 for a group of over 500 participants.

If you have questions about the online program, send an email to:

**Ingrid@facilitationtutor.com**

# Facilitator Certification

**Certified Professional Facilitator**

The top designation in the field is granted by the *International Association of Facilitators (IAF)*. This body conducts a review process that leads to the designation of *Certified Professional Facilitator (CPF)*.

The *CPF* process consists of the following steps: Applicants must have at least ten years experience as a group facilitator. Each applicant is asked to submit a paper describing six recent facilitation activities that they designed and led. Each facilitation case study cited must be accompanied by a signed letter from each of the clients mentioned. The applicant then attends a two-day assessment meeting in one of the cities posted on the *IAF* website. Locations change every six months or so. At the event, each applicant facilitates a complex discussion with a group of their fellow applicants. while a review panel observes. After a lengthy debriefing session, the panel decides whether or not to grant the *Certified Professional Facilitator* designation. The fee for taking part is approximately $1,500.00, plus the cost of travel and accommodation. To learn more about the *CPF* process go to www.iafworld.org.

**Validated Facilitator Certification**

Since the *CPF* process described above is accessible only to those who have been in practice for at least ten years, a more accessible certification process was created by *The Pfeiffer Company*, a leader in the development of tests and instruments. In 2009, they asked Ingrid Bens, the author of this book and the international best seller *Facilitating with Ease!,* to create a reliable test to assess facilitator competency. The result was the *Facilitation Skills Inventory (FSI)*.

The *FSI* is a test of twenty observable skills that must be mastered by all facilitators. To be assessed, all you need to do is find a facilitator colleague who is willing to observe you in action during a group meeting of at least one hour's length. After the meeting, the observer completes the inventory and offers specific feedback during a post-observation coaching session.

The *FSI* criteria yields results that show a facilitator to be at one of three levels: Developing, Accomplished. or Advanced. Because the *FSI* test was developed over three years with rigorous validation by a panel of certified professionals, these test results can be cited in resumes.

*The Facilitation Skills Inventory* is readily available on Amazon. If you want to be able to add a validated facilitation certification level to your next resume, simply purchase two of the FSI booklets: the *Participant Guide* and the *Observer Guide*, then find someone to observe and rate your performance. These cost approximately $25.00 each. You can also buy the instrument at www.wiley.com.

**Also by Ingrid Bens:**

**Individualized Education Program Meetings are vitally important!**

What's inside?
- an overview of facilitation basics, definitions, the essential core practices, tips about when and how to assume the neutral role
- chapters on decision-making tools and the effective use of questions
- dozens of process tools that bring structure and cohesion to conversations

The core of this book is organized around the specific facilitation tools that have been found to be effective at each of five distinct stages in the development of Individualized Education Programs.

For each stage, there's a short description of the purpose of that stage, the activities conducted and the challenges commonly encountered. For each stage, there's also a list of the most commonly made mistakes, the best practices and the facilitation tools that can be used to achieve optimal results.

Once you start applying these tools, you'll find that you won't want to run your Individualized Education Program meetings without them!

**Available on Amazon and other online book stores.**

# Annotated Bibliography

No single book can provide everything needed to conduct effective experiential learning. Since this book focuses mainly on the facilitation aspects, consider asking your school librarian to acquire some of the following excellent resources.

**101 Ways to Make Training Active** (2$^{nd}$ ed.) by Mel Silberman.
This is the ultimate handbook of engagement tools and techniques. Step-by-step instruction on how to design and use games, role plays and simulations. Easy to read and practical, with great examples. ISBN – 978-0878976125

**50 Creative Training Openers and Energizers** by Bob Pike and Lynn Salem.
An exhaustive compendium of fun, energetic activities to get students engaged by Bob Pike one of the most well-known experts in group dynamics. You can find inexpensive used copies online. ISBN – 978-0787953034

**Visual Meeting.** How Graphics, Sticky Notes and Idea Mapping Can Transform Group Productivity. Although this book was written for workplace teams, it's full of diagrams showing structured conversations in in picture form. A great way to learn how to make group leaning more engaging. ISBN-978-0-470-60178-5

**Teach Like a Pirate** by Dave Burgess
The most uplifting and inspirational book ever written about the benefits of engagement in the classroom. Full of sage advice from one of the pioneers of participative learning. ISBN-978-0-9882176-0-7

**Ditch That Textbook** by Matt Miller
Practical strategies to help you free your teaching and revolutionize your classroom. Full of examples about how to make training personal and make effective of technology. ISBN-978-0-9861554-0-6

**Learn Like A Pirate** by Paul Solarz
Strategies for creating a student-led classroom. This book is supported by an excellent website full of ideas for getting students to take responsibility for both their personal learning and for managing the classroom: www.learnlikeapirate.com ISBN-978-0-9882176-6-9

**www.MindTools.com**
This site describes every imaginable group conversation in step-by-step detail. It also features a vast number of questions to ask in a wide variety of situations. You can use most of it for free. If you really like it, ask your school to purchase an annual membership.

**The Big Book of Teambuilding Games** by JW. Newstrom and E. Scannell
An encyclopedia of teambuilding games and fun activities. Great ideas to energize you class every day. ISBN-0-07-046513-4.

## About the Author

**Ingrid Bens, M.Ed.,** is certified professional facilitator with over twenty-five years of experience as a consultant and trainer. Ingrid received a Master's Degree in Adult Education from the University of Toronto's, Faculty of Education *(OISE)*.

Ingrid is the well-known author of multiple bestselling books on the topic of facilitation. The best known is *Facilitating with Ease!* In 2009, Ingrid Bens was asked by Pfeiffer Publishing to create the *Facilitation Skills Inventory (FSI)*. This is currently the only validated instrument available for the assessment of facilitator competency. When she isn't consulting or writing, Ingrid Bens conducts workplace seminars on facilitation skills. In the past few years she has been conducting these workshops for teachers at both the primary and secondary grade levels.

## Contributors

Special thanks to the following educators who helped to ensure that this book was both practical and relevant.

**Martina K. Schmidt, PHD** has over 20 years of experience in the fields of education and financial management. Dr. Schmidt is an Instructor III of Finance and Real estate in the College of Business at the University of South Florida, St. Petersburg (USFSP), where she teaches both face-to-face and online under-graduate and graduate courses.

**Michael Spivey, MA, LPCA, NCC** holds a BA.in Spanish and History, an MA in Education and Human Development and an MA in Counseling. Michael Spivey is a certified professional facilitator who has served as a Facilitator assessor with The International Association of Facilitators. He currently teaches and serves as a counselor.

**Joe Marusic** is a secondary school vice-principal with the Greater Essex County District School Board in Ontario, Canada. He has a BA in Chemical Engineering, a Bain Education and an MBA. He has over ten years of experience using participative methods to teach high school mathematics.

**Sara Snowball** has a Master's Degree and TESOL Endorsement in Elementary Education and is certified to teach grades K-8. She has ten years of teaching in various school settings across a wide range of socio-economic levels, including Title I schools. Her specialty is creating tranquil and engaged classroom climates.

# Chapter References

**Chapter 1: Origins and Models**

Adult Education Association. *Adult Learning.* (1965) Adult Education Association. Washington, DC

Adult Education Association. *Processes of Adult Education.* (1965) Adult Education Association. Washington, DC.

Allender, J. S., "New Conceptions of the Role of the Teacher." *The Psychology of Open Teaching and Learning.* (1972) M.L. Silberman et al. Little Brown. Boston, MA.

Allman, P. & Mackie, K. J. (eds.) *Towards Developing a Theory of Andragogy.* (1983) University of Nottingham, Department of Adult Education. UK.

Bandura, A. *Social Learning Theory.* (1977) Prentice-Hall. Englewood Cliffs, NJ.

Brookfield, S. D., *Understanding and Facilitating Adult Learning.* (1986) Jossey-Bass, San Francisco, CA:

Brookfield, S. D. *Developing Critical Thinkers.* (1986) Jossey-Bass. San Francisco, CA.

Burney, Diana. *The Science of Learning.* D.C. (2014). National Institute for School Leadership (NISL). DC.

Entwhistle. N. *Styles of Learning and Teaching.* (1982) New York, NY.

Galbraith, Michael W. ed. *Adult Learning Methods.* 3$^{rd}$ ed. (2004) Krieger Publishing. Miami, Fl.

Knowles, M., *Holton, E. F., III; Swanson, R. A. The Adult Learner. (6th ed.). (2005).* Routledge, Burlington, MA.

Knowles, M. *The Modern Practice of Adult Education: From Pedagogy to Andragogy.* (1980) Association Press. Wilton, CT.

Miller, M. *Ditch That Textbook.* (2015) Burgess Consultants. San Diego, CA.

**Chapter 2: Facilitation Core Practices**

Argyris, C. *Intervention Theory and Method.* (1970) Addison-Wesley. Reading, MA.

Beckhard, R. *Organization Development: Strategies and Models.* (1969) Addison Wesley. Reading, MA.

Bennis, W.G. *Changing Organizations.* (1966) McGraw-Hill. New York.

Bens, Ingrid. *Facilitating with Ease!* 4$^{th}$ Edition (2018) Wiley. San Francisco, CA.

Bens, Ingrid. *The Facilitation Skills Inventory.* (2009) Pfeiffer. San Francisco, CA.

Block, P. *The Empowered Manager.* (1987) Jossey-Bass. San Francisco, CA.

Block, P. *Flawless Consulting* (2nd ed.). (1999) Pfeiffer. San Francisco, CA.

French, W.L., & Bell, C. H., Jr. *Organization Development.* (1978) Prentice Hall. Englewood Cliffs, N.J.

Hargrove, R. *Masterful Coaching.* (1995) Pfeiffer. San Francisco.

Hunter, Dale. *The Art of Facilitation*. (2007) Random House. New Zealand.

Jongewood, D. & James, M. *Winning with People*. (1973) Addison-Wesley. Reading, MA.

Lippitt, G.L. (*Organization Renewal*. 1969) Appleton, Century & Crofts. New York, NY.

McKroskey, J.C., Larson, C.E. & Knapp, M.L. *An Introduction to Interpersonal Communication*. (1971) Prentice Hall. Englewood Cliffs, N.J.

Nadler, D.A. *Feedback and Organization Development*. (1977) Addison-Wesley. Reading, MA.

Rees, F. *The Facilitator Excellence Handbook*. (1998) Jossey-Bass, San Francisco, CA.

Schein, E. H. *Process Consultation: Its Role in Organization Development*. (1969) Addison-Wesley. Reading, MA.

Schein, E. H. *Process Consultation: Lessons for Managers and Consultants*. (1987) Addison-Wesley. Reading, MA.

Schein, E. H. & Bennis, W. G., *Personal and Organization Change Through Group Methods: The Laboratory Approach*. (1965) John Wiley & Sons. Hoboken, N.J.

## Chapter 3: Effective Questioning

Fairhurst, G. & Sarr, R. *The Art of Framing*. (1996) Jossey-Bass. San Francisco. CA.

Harrison, R.,"Choosing the Depth of Organization Intervention." (1970) *The Journal of Applied Behavioral Science* 1 of 6, (2) 181-202.

Higgins, A. C. & Ashworth, S.D. *Organizational Surveys: Tools for Assessment and Change*. (1996) Jossey-Bass. San Francisco, CA.

Hogan, C. Practical Facilitation. (2003) Kogan-Page. Sterling, VA.

Hunter, D. *The Art of Facilitation*. (2007) Jossey-Bass. San Francisco, CA.

Schwarz, R. *The Skilled Facilitator*. (1994) Jossey-Bass. San Francisco, CA.

Stanfield, R. B. ed. *The Art of Focused Conversation*. (2000) ICA Toronto, Canada.

Strachen, D. *Questions That Work*. (2001) ST Pres. Ottawa, Canada.

Weisbord, M. R. *Organizational Diagnosis: A Workbook of Theory and Practice*. (1991) Jossey-Bass. San Francisco, CA.

## Chapter 4: Decision Making in the Classroom

Avery, M., Auvine, B., Streiel, B. & Weiss, L. *Building United Judgment: A Handbook for Consensus Decision Making*. (1981) The Center for Conflict Resolution. Madison, WI.

DeBono, E. *Six Thinking Hats*. (1985) Key Porter Books. Toronto, Canada.

DeBono, E., *Serious Creativity*. (1993) HarperCollins. New York, NY.

Fisher, A. B. *Small Group Decision Making: Communication and Group Process*. (1974) McGraw-Hill. New York, NY.

Fisher, R., & Ury, W. *Getting to Yes*. (1983) Penguin Books. New York, NY.

Hunter, Dale. *The Art of Facilitation.* (2007) Random House. New Zealand.

Kaner, S. *Facilitator's Guide to Participatory Decision-Making.* (1996) New Society Publishers. Philadelphia, PA.

Hunsaker, P. & Alessandra, A. *The Art of Managing People.* (1980) Prentice-Hall. Englewood Cliffs, N.J.

Kinlaw, D. C., *Team-Managed Facilitation.* (1993) Pfeiffer. San Francisco, CA.

Katzenbach, J. & Smith, D. *The Wisdom of Teams.* (1993) HarperCollins. New York, NY.

Kuhn, T. S. *The Structure of Scientific Revolutions.* (1970) University of Chicago Press. Chicago, IL.

Saint, S. & Lawson, J. R. *Rules for Reaching Consensus.* (1994) Jossey-Bass. San Francisco, CA.

Schneider, W. E. *The Reengineering Alternative: A Plan for Making Your Current Culture Work.* (1994) Irwin. Burr Ridge, Ill.

Van Gundy, A. B. Techniques of Structured Problem Solving. (1981) Van Nostrand Reinhold. New York, NY.

## Chapter 5: Facilitating Through Conflict

Beckhard, R. "The Confrontation Meeting." *Harvard Business Review.* March 1967, ed # 45. Boston, MA.

Beckhard, R. *Organization Development: Strategies and Models.* (1969) Addison-Wesley. Reading, MA.

Blake, R. R., Shepard, H. & Mouton, J. S. *Managing Intergroup Conflict in Industry.* (1965) Gulf Publishing. Houston, TX.

Filley, A. C., *Interpersonal Conflict Resolution.* (1975) Scott, Foresman. Ill.

Fisher, R. & Ury, W. *Getting to Yes.* (1983) Penguin Books. New York.

Kilmann, R. H. & Thomas, K. W. *Four Perspectives on Conflict Management: An Attributional Framework for Organizing Descriptive and Normative Theory.* (1978) Academy of Management Review.

Kindler, H. S. *Managing Disagreement Constructively.* (1988) Crisp Publications. Los Altos, CA

Levine S. *Getting Resolution: Turning Conflict Into Collaboration.* (1999) Berrett-Koehler. San Francisco, CA.

Lewin, K., & Hanson, P. "Giving Feedback: An Interpersonal Skill."

W. G. Bennis and others (eds.), *The Planning of Change* (3rd ed.) (1976) Holt Rinehart & Winston. New York.

Likert, R., & Likert, J. G. *New Ways of Managing Conflict.* (1976) McGraw-Hill. New York, NY.

Solarz, P., *Learn like a Pirate.* (2015) Burgess Consulting. San Diego, CA.

Thomas, K. W. & Kilmann, R. H. *The Thomas-Kilmann Conflict Mode Instrument.* (1974) Xicom. Tuxedo, N.Y.

*Facilitating in the Classroom*

Walton, R. E. *Managing Conflict: Interpersonal Dialogue and Third Party Roles.* (1987) Addison-Wesley. Reading, MA.

Zander, A. (1983) *Making Groups Effective.* Jossey-Bass. San Francisco.

**Chapter 6: Building Strong Teams**

Bens, I. (2005) *Team Launch.* Goal/QPC. Salem, NH.

Buchholz, S. & Roth, T. *Creating the High Performance Team.* (1987) John Wiley & Sons, New York, NY,

Dyer, W.G. *Team Building: Issues and Alternatives.* (1979) Addison-Wesley. Reading, MA.

Dyer, W. G. *Team Building.* 2nd ed. (1987) Addison-Wesley, Reading MA.

Carr, C. *Team Leader's Problem Solver.* (1996) Prentice Hall. New Jersey.

Katzenbach, J. and Smith, D., *The Wisdom of Teams.* (1993) Harper Collins. New York. NY

Leigh, A. and Maynard, M. *Leading Your Team.* (1995) Nicholas Brealey. UK.

Lencioni, P. *The Five Dysfunctions of Teams.* (2002) John Wiley and Sons, San Francisco, CA.

MacGregor, M. M. Teambuilding with Teams. (2008) Free Spirit Publishing. New York, NY.

Newstrom J.W. & Scannell, E. *The Big Book of Teambuilding Games.* (1997) McGraw-Hill. New York, NY.

Reddy, W.B.,*Team Building: Blueprints for Productivity and Satisfaction.* (1988) NTL Institute. Virginia.

Rees, F., *How to Lead Work Teams : Facilitation Skills.* (1991) Pfeiffer & Company. San Francisco. CA

Wellins, R.S.,Byham, W.C. & Wilson, J. M. *Empowered Teams.* (1991) Jossey-Bass. San Francisco.

**Chapter 7: Learning Design**

Bowman, S. *Preventing Death by Lecture.* (2001) Bowman Publishing, Glenbrook, NV.

Farber, D., Hines, A. & Hood, B. *Collaborating with Strangers.* (2017) American Library Association. Chicago, Ill.

Hunter, Dale. *The Art of Facilitation.* (2007) Random House. New Zealand.

Pike, Bob. *Creative Training Techniques Handbook.* 3$^{rd}$ ed. (2003) HRD Press. Amherst, MA.

Patrick Suessman. *Training Ideas Found Useful.*(1998) Paracan Publishing. Winnepeg, Canada.

Silberman, Mel. *101 Ways to make Training Active.* 2$^{rd}$ ed. (2010) Pfeiffer, San Francisco, CA.

Silberman, Mel., *Active Training.* 3$^{rd}$ ed. (2016) Pfeiffer, San Francisco, CA.

Thiagarajan, Sivasailam. *Design Your Own Games and Activities.* (2003) Pfeiffer, San Francisco, CA.

Wacker, M. & Silverman, Lori. *Stories Trainers Tell.* (2003) Pfeiffer, San Francisco, CA.

Wood, J. T., Phillips, G. M. & Pederson, D. J. *Group Discussion: A Practical Guide to Participation and Leadership* (2nd ed.) (1986). New York: Harper and Row.

## Chapter 8: Structured Conversations

Grove Consultants International. *Visual Meetings.* (2010) Wiley, New Jersey.

Kaufman, R. *Identifying and Solving Problems.* (1976) University Associates. San Diego CA.

Pfeiffer, J. W. & Jones, J. E. *A Handbook of Structured Experiences for Human Relations Training* (vols 1 -X). (1972) San Francisco, CA.

Pfeiffer, J. W. & Jones, J. E. *A Handbook of Structured Experiences for Human Relations Training* (vols 1 -X). (1972) San Francisco, CA.

Stanfield, R. B., ed. *The Art of Focused Conversation.* (2000) ICA Canada. Toronto, Canada.

Van Gundy, A. B. *Techniques of Structured Problem Solving.* (1981) Van Nostrand Reinhold. New York, NY.

## Buy In Quantity and Save!

If you're thinking of buying this book or others by Ingrid Bens, for a large group, email for a better price. We can drop ship any quantity. Group purchases start at 10 books.

| | |
|---|---|
| 1 - 9 copies | $32.00 |
| 10 – 99 copies | 25% discount |
| 100 - 249 copies | 30% discount |
| 250 - 499 copies | 35% discount |
| 500 and up | Contact us for a quote |

### Make It Your Own

Include your motto, mission and logo on the outside and inside covers, even add a page with your personal message. We can also create a custom front and back cover for a fee. Drop us an email at the address below to request the full details of customization.

**Ingrid@facilitationtutor.com**